Generis

PUBLISHING

i

Investigation of Project Delays in Construction Projects in the South African Rail Industry

Itumeleng G. Motlhatlhedi

CIP a Camerei Naționale a Cărții

Motlhatlhedi, Itumeleng G.

Investigation of Project Delays in Construction Projects in the South African Rail Industry / Itumeleng G. Motlhatlhedi. – Chişinău : Generis Publishing, 2020 (Print on demand). – 98 p. : fig. color, tab.

Referințe bibliogr.: p. 81-86.

ISBN 978-9975-154-24-6.

625.1/.5(680)

M 92

Cover image: www.pixabay.com

Publisher: Generis Publishing

Online orders: www.generis-publishing.com

Orders by email: info@generis-publishing.com

Acknowledgements

In preparation of this book, sundry input was required from various individuals. I would like to extend my gratitude to all of them.

First, my sincere gratitude to Dr Hannelie Nel, who was firm, honest and professional. I would not have accomplished this study without her unwavering support.

Secondly, I would like to thank the questionnaire survey respondents for their contribution. Without their involvement, the research would not have been successful.

In addition, a huge thank you to my colleagues at R&H Rail (Pty) Limited for covering for me in my absence.

To my editor, Ms Liza Marx from Academic and Professional Editing Services (APES), for attending to proofreading and copy-editing of my study.

Abstract

The construction industry is one of the largest contributing sectors towards the Gross Domestic Product of countries globally, and South Africa is no exception. The construction industry in South Africa and globally, are marred with extensive delays. This is a persisting enduring challenge.

This study investigated the project delay factors in construction projects, particularly the Passenger Rail Agency of South Africa and Transnet traction substation projects in the South African railway engineering environment. The research also presented the remedial actions and mitigations suitable to be implemented to manage project delays in the project engineering environment.

The research was conducted through a literature review and a questionnaire survey. The deductive research approach was employed. An online questionnaire survey was used to collect primary data. The literature review summary revealed eight top project delay-causing factors in traction substation projects, forming the basis of the questionnaire.

The questionnaire results correlated with the literature review. This dissertation proposed suitable measures to manage delays in construction projects, improving the quality of work, and to manage cost and schedule overruns.

Keywords: project delays, construction industry, project management.

Table of Contents

List of Figures

List of Tables

List of Abbreviations

APES	Academic and Professional Editing Services
BBBEE	Broad-Based Black Economic Empowerment
BPM	Business process modelling
CAA	Civil Aviation Authority
COD	College of DuPage
CSU	Case Study University
DoT	Department of Transport
MBA	Masters Degree in Business Administration
MBL	Masters Degree in Business Leadership
Mtpa	Million tonnes per annum
NDP	National Development Plan
OHTE	Overhead Traction Equipment
PRASA	Passenger Rail Agency of South Africa
GDP	Gross Domestic Product
HV	High Voltage
NTR	External or Nontechnical Risks
OSF	Off-Site Fabrication
PMP	Project Management Professional
ROB	Road Over Bridge
R&H	Robertson & Hitchins Railway Consultants
SA	Strongly Agree
SD	Strongly Disagree
TFR	Transnet Freight Rail
TQM	Total Quality Management
UK	United Kingdom
UAE	United Arab Emirates

Chapter 1
Introduction and Background

1.1 Introduction

In the modern era, the construction industry immensely offers and contributes towards the global economy through employing and developing an infrastructure. Project delays are major challenges, hindering the successful completion of several construction projects (Srdic and Selih, 2015).

Quality, time and cost are considered as the three requirements to be met for a project to be regarded successful. It has been a perception in the construction industry, that time as a crucial parameter selected from the three aforementioned parameters, mostly evaluates the success of the project (Ansah and Shahryar, 2018).

Globally and for South Africa, the main objective of the South African construction industry is to complete projects within the agreed budget and schedule. The aim is also to complete projects accident free, maintaining high standards and quality. The delays during the design and planning phases of the project hold dire consequences on the project construction schedule, resulting in unrealistic deliverables and timelines. Yang and Wei (2010) state that it is of utmost importance to identify factors that hinder the critical project path, and to resolve project delays.

According to Kazaz, Ulubeyli and Tuncbilekli (2012), project performance is heavily affected by delays experienced in the project. The client is entitled to alterations if they sense that they are not receiving value for their money. It has proved to be difficult though, to set boundaries concerning amendments from clients (which they are entitled to), since certain clients suggest alterations towards the end of the project, causing huge delays.

Hussain, Zhu, Ali, and Xu (2017) mentioned that termination of contracts, disputes, extension of time schedules, interrupted work, budget overrun, and unhappy clients, contribute to project delays. Events in the project engineering environment suggest that it is becoming custom for several construction projects to attempt to remedy the problem of project delays by spending more funds (contingency) to accelerate and fast-track the project. These endeavours aim to meet the set milestones, such as adding more resources to the project or working overtime. Nielsen, Özdemir and Gündüz (2013) suggest that the norm of relying on contingency has set a bad precedent in the project environment to solve project delay challenges.

Soliman (2017) mentions that inadequate communication appears to be the main source of disputes and conflicts in construction projects globally. Failure to communicate effectively amongst the project stakeholders, such as clients, consultants and contractors, often leads to unsuccessful project results, incurring cost and schedule overruns due to delays and rework on the project. According to Soliman (2017), successful projects in the construction industry employs good and effective communication practices across all the project stakeholders.

Soliman (2017) mentions that the research performed at Kuwait, a country situated in Western Asia, revealed the top five ranked communication problems causing delays in Kuwait Government projects:

- The previous outdated document filing system was still in use and the Government was resistant to change their filing system and adopt new technologies;
- Site meetings were not held consistently, disabling tracking of the progress on site activities;
- Delays in approving construction documents, such as construction drawings by the client;
- The appointment of in-experienced supervision personnel to manage the construction activities on behalf of Government (client); and
- Inadequate quality of the design drawings and other documents for construction (Soliman, 2017).

It is a widespread belief in the project environment that all the project stakeholders require hassle free projects. Several researchers, such as Williams (2016), Spalek, S. (2005) and Zakaria *et al.* (2017) conducted studies on project success factors. They found out that, the project is considered successful if the final product is good, stakeholders are satisfied and if the delivery objectives are met. The team selection for a project is a crucial factor (Duke, 2016) that could either make or break the project. Williams (2016) postulates that the iron triangle, comprising time, quality and cost, are the considered factors determining the project's failure or success.

With the conclusion of the project, the typical questions raised (or the evaluation criteria that the project owners use) include: Assessing whether the objectives of the project were met, paying special attention to the set timelines and the funds spent on the project (Williams, 2016). The client also evaluates the quality of the product and the professionalism of the services rendered by the contractor or service provider. Williams (2016) further states that the project is more likely to be considered successful if the stakeholders are satisfied, particularly if the client sees value for their money and if the contractor profits. Project managers always aim to accomplish project completion with zero harm to humans or animals, zero defects and minimum disruptions.

Rao *et al.* (2016) studied construction delays. They conclude that delays are general challenges in the industry and they are costly. They can only be dealt with if their causes are identified. Sources of the construction delays often emanate from the disagreements between the significant participants in a project, which include the contractor, client and the consultant.

The study by Rao *et al.* (2016) summarises delays into four types, whereby delays are described to be compensable or non-compensable, critical or non-critical and can occur simultaneously or at different periods during the project. The study postulated that some construction delays are justifiable, and others are non-justifiable. Delays caused by weather conditions are justifiable. Delays caused by rework because the contractor is in-experienced, are non-justifiable (Rao *et al.*, 2016).

Parsons (2015) investigated the causes for incomplete large construction projects within the pre-set time limits, according to the project schedule. The author believes that the public had the right to be told why major construction projects often experience delays, by exposing the project delay-causing factors to the public. The study mentions that the greatest problem in the project environment, often leading to disputes and litigations, is misaligned expectations. Parsons (2015) performed the research in Canada. The emphasis was on large construction projects, such as building of airports, renovating the Nathan Phillip Square, the Calgary airport that was supposed to be expanded and constructing the Johnson Street Bridge and highway construction projects.

The general observation in these projects is that they failed to meet the construction deadlines and they incurred cost overruns of 50% on average. About 109 interviews were conducted with the project stakeholders in Europe, Asia, the Middle East and Africa to ascertain delay causes in construction projects.

Consultants and contractors often tend to accept more projects (more work), even if they do not have the capacity to execute the projects, with the view of securing work for the next season (Parsons, 2015). Hiring of in-experienced contractors and consultants, unrealistic designs by the engineering team, political interference, extreme weather conditions and appointing a contractor because they present the lowest bid, often lead to failure of the project (Parsons, 2015).

1.2   Background

A reliable transport infrastructure is fairly influential and significant in generating economic growth for several countries globally. It has the potential to increase global and domestic competitiveness, alleviate poverty and to create jobs through transport infrastructure development projects. For the past few years, the South African railway industry focussed on commuter trains and transportation of freight.

The Passenger Rail Agency of South Africa (PRASA) and Gautrain are well-known commuter train companies in the country within the railway engineering industry. Transnet is South Africa's freight transportation operator, comprising five operational divisions, with Transnet Freight Rail (TFR) being its largest division. South Africa's Department of Transport (DoT) is responsible for legislation and policies within the railway industry. PRASA and Transnet are State Owned Enterprises (SOEs) and their rail network spreads throughout the country, powered by more than 500 traction substations for each company on their networks, respectively.

South Africa continues to embark on railway infrastructure development projects, based on technological changes, railway industrial evolutional and increasing customer demands (Miller *et al.*, 2017). Most of these projects are in line with South Africa's National Development Plan (NDP) as passed and accepted by the National Assembly as one of the strategic plans for the country to generate and stimulate economic growth.

These railway infrastructure development projects entail building new traction substations, upgrading and refurbishing the existing stations, and upgrading the Overhead Traction Equipment (OHTE).

The rail transport system is still considered as the most efficient mode of transport for commuter traffic and bulk freight. This is despite the sophisticated and modern modes of transportation. Moving freight off the roads to the railway, minimise trucks on the roads, reduce road traffic and accidents, and the overhead costs are low since modern trains are mostly powered with electricity, which is cheaper than fuel used by trucks on the road.

Transnet embarked on infrastructure development projects to increase its railway network throughput to 81Mtpa, to provide export freight and commuter transportation capacity in line with the industry demand into the future, with a view to expanding this capacity to 91Mtpa. This aspirational volume was based on the estimates from the industry. The risk was that ultimate export coal volume requirements could vary, but the 81Mtpa target was agreed upon (Miller *et al.*, 2017).

TFR assets currently include over 2000 locomotives, operating on three HV distribution systems. The three HV distribution systems used in South Africa, are 3kV DC, 25kV AC and 50kV AC. Figure 1 depicts the railway network for various voltage systems in South Africa.

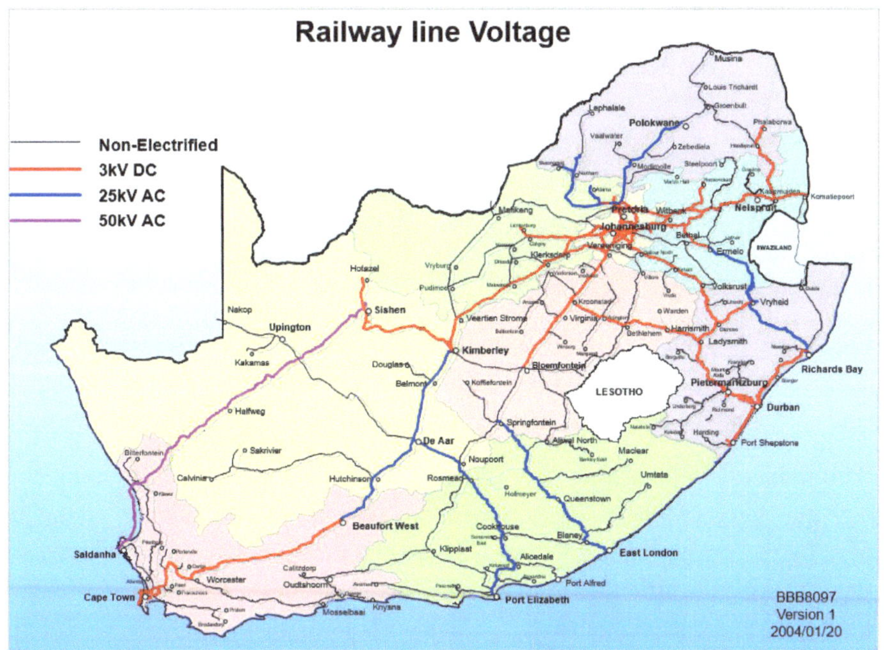

Figure 1: South African Railway Network, Transnet Freight Rail, Drawing No. BBB8097, Sheet 1 of 1 (2004)

It was proposed that the electrical energy supply network be expanded as necessary, including traction substations, to allow for an increase in annual coal export volumes to 81Mtpa. This will provide additional capacity, allowing for the planned ramp-up of coal transportation.

Figure 2 depicts the lifecycle of traction substations from Phase one to six.

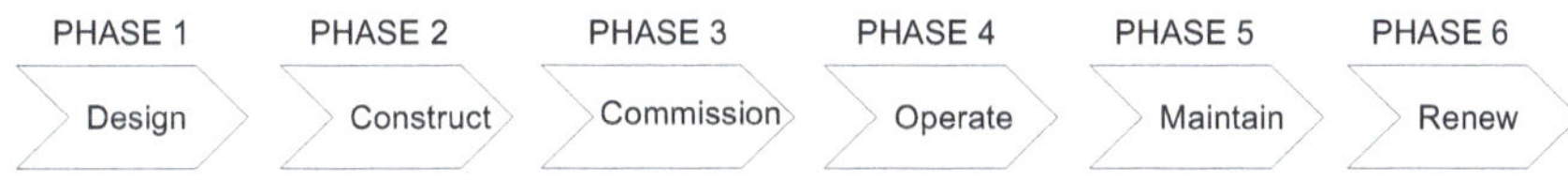

Figure 2: Lifecycle Phases of Traction Substations

Traction substation projects comprise the first three phases of the lifecycle of traction substations, including design, construction and commissioning phases. These phases of traction substation projects determine the operating philosophy of the substation and maintainability in a sense that the project specification guides the contractor on which equipment to install, as instructed by the asset owner.

1.3   Motivation for the Study

The South African economy has been unstable and on the decline over the past few years. The country was recently downgraded to 'junk' status (Suzman Foundation, 2016). Previous studies r that the construction industry is a crucial participant in the economy of any country (globally) as it creates employment for the citizens and generates wealth for the country, particularly concerning the infrastructure development (Miller *et al.*, 2017).

The study's objective was to identify causes of project delays and the impact thereof, ultimately proposing the mitigations that could be implemented to deal with this dilemma hindering the construction industry.

1.4   Importance/Significance of the Study

To complete a project timeously and ensure cost saving, is considered to be the main objective by the project stakeholders. The stakeholders comprise the project owner, contractor and other participants. Several factors result in more project costs, delays in the schedule and legal disputes.

The significance of this study was to research a global problem, indicating delays in construction projects continuing to worsen. The study also aimed to gain an in-depth underlying theoretical understanding of the subject through questionnaire surveys and conducting a literature review in the pursuit to propose suitable mitigation measures.

1.5   Problem Statement

The construction industry is marred with project delays, both in South Africa and globally (Marks and Ellis, 2017). Too many construction projects are delayed, due to schedule overruns, resulting in negative cost implications (Nkobane, 2012) and (Abdul-Rahman, Takim and Min, 2009).

Project delays in the construction industry continue to derail several projects. This research focussed on causes of delays on selected traction substation construction projects that Transnet and the Passenger Rail Agency of South Africa (PRASA) undertook and embarked on.

1.6   Research Questions

The research questions are stated as follows:

- What causes delays in traction substation projects within railway engineering?
- What mitigation plans could be implemented to manage project delays?

1.7   Purpose of the Study

This research aimed to ascertain critical factors causing delays in the project environment and their impact. The study aimed to identify the mitigations that may be applied to improve the construction industry.

1.8   Research Objectives

The objective of the research was to investigate the factors causing project delays in construction projects and to identify suitable measures to be implemented to manage project delays in the construction industry.

1.9   The Research Structure

The principle focus of this research was to ascertain causes and impact of project delays in the construction industry, specifically traction substation projects within railway engineering.

The literature review is discussed in Chapter 2, paying special attention to previous research on the topic. Chapter 3 articulates and unpacks the research methodology for study. Emphasis is place on the research approach, research limitations, envisaged results and ethical considerations. The definition of modes of data collection is detailed in the research methodology section.

These methods, described in the methodology, define the means or modes of data collection. The calculation of a specific result is described. Chapter 4 presents the collected data and the analyses thereof. The discussion of the findings, conclusion and remedial actions or recommendations, are structured and articulated in Chapter 5 and Chapter 6 respectively. The collected data derived through questionnaire surveys, were analysed and are discussed in detail in this chapter.

The discussions entail establishing if the literature review and questionnaire survey addressed the research questions that guided the study. The chapter presents the analyses of the factual matter of the results and does not seek to indicate the implications thereof. The information pertaining statistical procedure also forms part of Chapter 4.

The crucial focus areas for Chapter 5, are the interpretation and description of results or findings concerning previous knowledge on the research problem investigated. The chapter presents and explains the innovative understanding and perspective, after assessing the research findings.

1.10 Chapter Summary

The aforementioned research questions were answered through the literature review in Chapter 2 and the questionnaire survey conducted. The data collection was analysed and compared to the reviewed literature. Suitable mitigation measures are recommended at the conclusion of this study.

Chapter 2

Literature Review

2.1   Introduction

The literature review in this minor dissertation aimed to study relevant information sources, including books, peer-reviewed journals and articles relevant to the topic in question, identifying causes and impacts of project delays in traction substation projects. The process offered an explanation, summary, and critical evaluation of these works concerning the research problem under investigation. In this chapter, the literature review structure aims to offer an overview of sources explored whilst researching the aforementioned topic. It demonstrates how the research fits within a larger field of study. The literature review provides a new interpretation of previous study material. It also combines innovative with previous interpretations, identifying the divergences in topic related researches.

2.2   Overview of the Construction Industry/Sector on Project Delays

The strong economic position for several countries globally, revolves around investing in the construction industry (Miller *et al.*, 2017). (Ofori-Kuragu *et al.*, 2016) revealed that investing in infrastructure development projects, ensures growing of the economy of the country because of job creation, improved services to individuals or consumers, improvement in global and domestic competitiveness and poverty alleviation.

Based on comprehensive literature, a holistic view on the Gross Domestic Product (GDP) of several global countries in the agricultural and construction sectors, often appear as the leading top two main contributors. Their contributions indicate 10% (Ofori-Kuragu *et al.*, 2016). The construction industry are marred with delays and this enduring problem persists. Several researchers conducted various studies in a quest to address this challenge reaching epidemic proportions.

Global construction institutions acknowledge that the industry suffers from abandoned project, cost and schedule overruns, poor performance and several other difficulties, hindering successful project delivery. Amoatey and Ankrah (2017) postulate that uncontrolled factors, such as weather conditions, disrupt the project schedule. Other challenges emanate from technical, political, social, environmental and economic issues.

History suggest that project delays were always part of construction projects. The difference between the past and the present is the accelerated rate of project delays. Several industry experts and researchers who conducted studies on the subject such as Duke (2015) and Stoudt (2013), recommend implementing improved project management practices and employing good engineering ethics.

2.3   Causes of Project Delays

Several studies attempted to analyse, investigate and identify critical factors that directly or indirectly hinder the progress of construction project. These factors consequently cause projects to fail to meet the completion stage within the pre-set timelines.

The economy is heavily influenced by the construction industry; it has the capability to generate both wealth and employment to individuals (Sweis *et al.*, 2008). It is widely observed that delays occur in both complex and simple construction projects. Several studies revealed that some project delays are caused by situations beyond human control, such as weather conditions.

Yang, Chu and Huang (2013) mention that delays in the project schedule are typically due to late scope changes by the client or the developer and the design changes by the engineers or late delivered drawings. The State indicates that some delays are caused by the unavailability of industry experts or limited time when they are needed to approve or inspect the project output, and poor multidisciplinary interface on the designs and on site.

Environmental condition factors, such as extreme temperatures were debated subjects over the years by several expects. Several developers fail to make provision for these factors in the project schedule, as it is unpredictable.

The gas and oil projects in Alberta were marred with delays, cost overruns and schedule overruns (Chanmeka *et al.*, 2012). Research was conducted to identify causes and factors affecting the productivity and performance of these projects. The perception indicated the main reason for poor project performance as inadequate labour productivity.

Chanmeka *et al.* (2012) indicate that thirty-seven gas and oil projects in Alberta were investigated and analysed. The authors state that the necessity of this study was because of the uncertainty in the industry. No empirical research was conducted previously to validate the anecdotal conclusions, identifying labour productivity as the cause of project failures in Alberta.

The research revealed that inadequate labour productivity was merely a proximate cause of project delays. The main causes of project delays and poor project performance included the following:

- Poor project planning.
- Inaccurate or erroneous cost estimations.
- Mega projects - resource shortages, skilled labourers.
- Poor execution plans for projects - improper interfacing.
- Scope creeps.
- Incorrect engineering designs and employing former technologies; late submission of engineering designs/ deliverables.
- A lack of best management practices (Chanmeka *et al.*, 2012).

The projected cost growth on the project is calculated by subtracting the project cost initially predicted from the actual total project cost, dividing the difference by the initial project cost. Similarly, the difference after subtracting the phase cost initially predicted from the actual phase cost, is the method used to calculate phase cost growth (Chanmeka *et al.* 2012).

According to Chanmeka *et al.* (2012), the scope change factor could be estimated by dividing the value of scope changes' total cost by the actual total project. The study further indicates calculating the total change cost factor may be accomplished by dividing the sum of the total scope cost changes and development changes by the actual total project cost.

The construction phase of the project is crucial, and it affects the total cost of the project by 35% to 50%, making it the main driver of the project (Rentschler *et al.*, 2017). During the project risk assessment, construction feasibility is often considered as the deciding factor, determining whether the project should be concluded or embarked. Other project costs include engineering cost, which is likely to be in the range of 10% to 15% of the total cost.

The procurement costs are significantly higher than engineering costs because they include purchasing of equipment and materials needed for the project; they are directly dependent on the engineering design (Rentschler *et al.*, 2017). This means that the bill of quantities is generated from the quantities detailed in the engineering designs. Improper project feasibility studies and collection of inadequate data and improper surveys prior to the design, often hinder the project construction progress. This occasionally leads to abandoning or failure of the project.

Rentschler *et al.* (2017) indicate that it is a challenging task to quantify construction costs for the project because of unforeseen circumstances that may arise during the construction stage. A way to attempt to quantify construction costs for a project, is to embark on a detailed labour survey; this is generally considered a laborious and tedious exercise. Engagements with the local experienced, knowledgeable, qualified contractors are apprehended for a provided geography.

Rentschler *et al.* (2017:32) further mentioned that small projects are more puzzling and challenging than mega projects. This is purely because the duration of these projects is shorter and the margin for error tend to be low. Another contributing factor is a trend in the industry, observing that the project team tends to be complacent, take small projects for granted and fail to pay attention to detail concerning designs and costs. Alternative project aspects are concerned, leading to schedule and cost overruns.

According to Rentschler *et al.* (2017:32), transactions were previously negotiated on 'a handshake', which is impractical. Contractors are always contemplating ways to maximise their profit. The project developer is always attempting to reduce their costs by reducing their expenditure. The introduction of conducting business through signed contractual agreements encourages project stakeholders to act in good faith. Improved project performance and performance output could be accomplished if the relationship between the contractor and the client is sensible with mutual respect. This aspect reduces the chances of litigations, encouraging future partnerships.

The overruns and delays in construction projects are often caused by low productivity, pressed schedules, outsourcing, shortage of qualified works, complex projects, non-compliance to regulations, complex contract agreements or arrangements and adoptions of new technologies (Rentschler *et al.*, 2017).

The construction industry in Alberta, in the Western province in Canada, are growing tremendously, contributing to the growth of the country's economy. Previous studies revealed that numerous megaprojects were subjected to cost and schedule overruns. An observation from earlier studies, identifies the rework as a main contributing factor to the continued challenge of project delays and overruns (Aminah, Manjula and Oswaldo, 2004). Researchers determined the relationship between the project rework and resulting adverse implications on the cost and schedule of the project.

Ghana is one of the African developing countries. Earlier studies submitted that the country's construction industry contributes 8.2% to the its GDP (Ofori-Kuragu *et al.*, 2016). The construction industry in Ghana was under scrutiny for the past few years, due to failure of delivering infrastructure development projects timeously and within a budget. Unsubstantiated conclusions stated that contractors were to blame for problems and hardships experienced in the construction sector. The authors further postulate that the Ghana statistics indicate that the overrun on cost in projects typically range from 60% to 180%. Construction projects indicate average delays of one to two years.

Ofori-Kuragu *et al.* (2016) conducted a research on the case of construction industry council in Ghana. Through an empirical study, the following factors were identified as major contributors to poor performance in the Ghanaian construction industry:

- The engineering sector in the country is insufficiently capacitated - several large projects tend to be awarded to foreign companies.
- There is lack of funding for projects. When the funding becomes available, the interest rate is often extremely high.
- Payment delays to contractors and consultants - Ghanaian contractors often protest to demand payments post completion of projects.
- Burdensome and cumbersome processes of payments.
- Political interference on the awarding of construction tenders.
- Awarding tenders to in-experienced, disreputable and newcomer companies.

Delays in the construction industry indicate global widespread problems; most of them are caused by design errors, poor contract administration and a lack of client supervision (Ali and Rahmat, 2010). This led to schedule and cost overruns, litigations, disputes, variations from the original scope of work and abandoned projects.

Venkateswaran and Murugasan (2017) studied The Road over Bridge (ROB) construction projects. Their aim was to identify factors contributing to cost and schedule overruns. Sixty-two individuals, including consultants, asset owners and contractors took part in the questionnaire survey. Records identified 29 factors as major contributors to construction delays of ROB project delays in India.

The findings by Venkateswaran and Murugasan (2017) revealed that in most cases, contractors and consultants underestimate the complexity of the ROB projects. Subsequently low bid prices are offered, only to realise in the duration of the project that the requirements are more than what was planned.

The identified contributing delay factors encompassed, the acquisition of land, incapacitated and in-experienced contractors, relocation of the existing services from site to commence with the project, failure to grant site access to the contractor timeously and long turnaround time for permit approval (Venkateswaran and Murugasan, 2017).

Zidane and Andersen (2018) investigated causes of delays in Norwegian projects, and suitable measures to be implemented to remedy the situation. According to the findings of the study, the top causes of delays included:

(1) workers' low productivity; (2) insufficient availability of construction equipment; (3) complex designs, requiring more time; (4) payment delays by the client; (5) mismanagement of funds by the contractor; (6) favouring lowest bid prices over experienced and reputable contractors; and (7) interference from politics (Zidane and Andersen, 2018).

Zidane and Andersen (2018) conducted a questionnaire survey as part of their research methodology; 202 respondents in Norway participated. The questionnaire was structured to capture the background information and the employment details of respondents, recording three major delay factors from each participant. Respondents also provided their views on how construction project delays could be managed for the current and future Norwegian projects.

2.4   Impact of Project Delays: Quality, Time and Cost

Abdul-Rahman *et al.* (2006) state that construction project delays is not a peculiar challenge but a general phenomenon. If project completion occurs after the agreed dates on the project schedule, it has negative cost implications on the project. The delays in the project are observed to be a costly predicament. The delays vary from project to project; it could be hours, days, weeks or even years, but that does not necessary indicate the extend of financial loss incurred. It is possible that the project that was delayed by a few hours, suffered a severe financial crisis, exceeding a project that was suspended for a year; it is generally considered in such a dynamic field.

R.D. Olson Construction (2014) discussed the negative implications that delay a construction project and mentioned what the project owners could anticipate when faced with litigation. The research postulates that if the client is a source of delays in a project, conversely, if the project owner is responsible for the delays, the contractor is entitled to claim overheads. The contractor may claim for the extended site work, such as additional supervision. They may be required to hire machinery or equipment on site, charged per hour, day or a specific period. This is likely to cost more than indicated in the original budged, due to delays.

According to R.D. Olson Construction (2014), the cost to run a business could be charged by the contractor during litigation, to pay taxes, salaries and insurance amongst others. The contractor could also claim an overtime post litigation process in an effort to compensate for the lost production time, due to delays caused by the project owner.

The application of lean tools in the project environment could be the answer to minimise or reduce project delays (Oakland and Marosszeky, 2017). Project management techniques and conventional project management concepts lack strength and clear direction to decisively solve delays in construction projects. Lean and six sigmas, off-site fabrication (OSF), total quality management (TQM), business process modelling (BPM) and prefabrication, amongst others, indicate the approaches in the project engineering sector and construction industry. These were implemented to manage delays in construction projects.

Project delays can be classified into four categories, indicating: Origin, compensability, timing and impact (Srdic and Selih, 2015). Based on the contents of the journal, delays have the origin, indicating there is always the owner, the person responsible for the delays. Certain delays are justifiable, such as harsh weather conditions; some delays are unjustifiable, such as delays caused by poor planning. Certain delays can occur concurrently, and some can occur non-concurrently. Certain delays might have a direct impact on the project, such as instigating negative financial implications on the project, whereas some indirectly influence the project.

In the view of Marks and Ellis (2017), factors such as a rapid increase in the price of materials, extended durations to approve the designs, long lead items not procured timeously, changes to the original scope of projects, improper pre-feasibility studies, regular breakdown of machinery on site and labour unrests, contribute to construction project delays.

Gluszak and Lesniak (2015) suggest that it is in the best interest of the client and the contractor to complete the construction work within the scheduled time. The responsibility of project managers are enormous; they have to coordinate the tasks, engage stakeholders, observe the cash flow and chair meetings, amongst others. Project delays are often kept to a minimum if the project team is united and proactive.

Time is a crucial or crucial factor concerning project engineering; it became a norm in the construction industry, evaluating the project success or failure by observing whether completion deadlines were met (Aziz, 2013). Globally, industrial construction projects, including traction substations, continue to suffer because of delays. A significant contributing factor to this widespread problem is the management of material. Delays experienced in the construction project supply chain are causing major deviations from the construction schedule; even small delays in the manufacture's works may have massive negative implications on the construction schedule.

Communication between the suppliers and contractors appear to be a problematic aspect. Certain studies revealed that several suppliers tend to inform the contractors close to the planned delivery date, concerning the expected delays (Aziz, 2013).

According to Wang and Hubbarb (2017), the construction material in an industrial project involves 50% to 60% of the project budget. Efficient management of material, including procurement and timeous placement of orders suggest that it is most likely for the project to be a success, completed on time and within the projected budget. The phenomenon of the Bullwhip effect continues to put strain on the management of materials in construction projects. The Bullwhip effect suggests that the companies in the supply chain need to order more goods to meet new demands for changes, prompted by consumers from time to time.

The residents in certain rural areas in Pakistan, participated in a study aiming to learn and capture their insights and observations concerning causes of project delays within the construction industry in their area. The study focussed on and evaluated the project delay causes because of socio-economic influencing factors. The project delay factors are classified into eight top critical categories (Hussain *et al.*, 2017). The ranking of the project delay causes from one to eight was based on the feedback from respondents from the rural areas in Pakistan, through a questionnaire survey methodology. The rankings are in a numerical order from one to eight as follows (Hussain *et al.*, 2018:10):

- Contractors' difficulties to manage the project funds:

Research suggests it is likely for project delays to occur as most contractors depend on progress payments from the clients to keep their doors open and their business operational. Conversely in some instances, contractors were found to fail to maintain a positive cash flow because of mismanagements of funds and were occasionally unable to tie the schedule activities with the cash flow.

- Delay in progress payments:

The study indicates that overdue payments to contractors hold severe repercussions on the project. Contractors rely on progress payments to procure materials, pay staff wages and other services needed.

- Dispute on land usage:

The issue of privately owned land appeared to be a sensitive issue. In some areas the communities and traditional leaders refuse compensation or to sell a piece of land to allow a construction project to commence, because of traditional beliefs and cultures, such as claiming that a particular area is their ancestral land and therefore it is sacred.

Farming was identified as a problem area, because most farmers are often sceptical to sell their land for a project due to agricultural reasons, especially during the drought periods and harsh economic times.

- Improper project feasibility study:

The studies further indicate that improper feasibility studies for the construction project remains a huge obstacle, causing disruptions in the project. Should geotechnical studies and load flow (or power flow) simulations not be conducted properly, prior to the commencement of the project, the contractor awarded the tender, is most likely to experience challenges, such as drainage issues, land disputes and inadequate power supply amongst others, during construction.

- Award the project to the lowest bid price:

It is perceived to be a substantial risk to award a construction project tender to the lowest bidder. Studies indicate that occasionally the reason the pricing is low, is because the tenderer or the bidder is unaware or does not understand the extent of the project. Some contractors bid at a lower price, but they compromise the quality of the work to maximise their profits. Another issue that enters the fray relates to poor conformance towards good engineering ethics as governed by the engineering council concerning low bid prices. In this regard, delays are most likely to be caused by inspectors who discontinue the construction activities due to poor quality performance and non-conformance to the engineering standards.

- Extreme weather conditions:

Unfavourable weather conditions such as severe cold or hot weather and the seasonal rainfalls, are often referred to as major delay factors in the construction environment. Despite the weather forecast conducted during the project planning phase, from time to time the weather forecast are miscalculated or misinterpreted. Such conditions are beyond control and are often dealt with as and when they occur, consequently putting strain on the project schedule.

- Inadequate contractor experience:

Research indicates that several developing countries are focussing on empowering small engineering companies by awarding them tenders as part of Broad-Based Black Economic Empowerment (BBBEE). Some of these strategies, indicated to stimulate the country's growth and reduce unemployment rate, also seem to be influence mediocrity and poor quality of work by in-experienced contractors in the construction industry. In-experienced contractors tend to disobey the safety regulations and engineering standards and often learn on the job, resulting in delays.

- Unsatisfactory survey before design and collection of inadequate data:

In some projects, the client fail to collect all the necessary site information before issuing a tender in the market. several contractors file claims and lawsuits against the client during project construction, because occasionally they under-price or undercharge because they were not provided with all the relevant information. For instance, the contractor might only realise during construction that the allocated site for the project is a rocky area. Hussain *et al*. (2017) developed a conceptual model where the impact of infrastructure projects on rural communities is depicted.

Amoatey and Ankrah (2017) states that construction projects are crucial to the economic and social development in several developing countries. Project delays in construction projects somewhat hindered this economic and social development and thus causing inconveniencies, such as cost overruns, increased construction period and bad reputation.

Delays in construction projects often result in over expenditure, disagreements or lawsuits. Certain projects are abandoned. In general, construction project delays are perceived as the most familiar, intricate and widespread challenge in the construction industry (Amoatey and Ankrah, 2017). Figure 3 indicates the conceptual model depicting how the Parkistan government would evaluate the impact of project delays on economic and social conditions of the rural community.

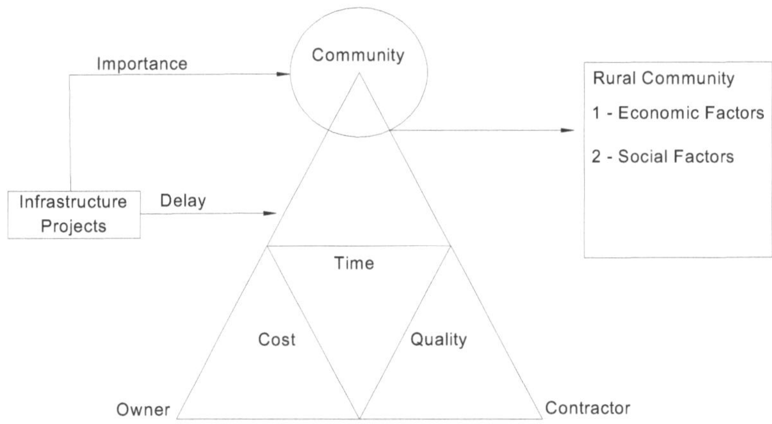

Figure 3: Conceptual Model (Hussain et al., 2017:4)

The study by Amoatey and Ankrah (2017) further highlights that delays might be caused by either internal or external factors. The stakeholders, including the contractors, consultant and the client, were identified as primary sources of delays from within the project. The external causes are considered as factors outside the control of the project, such as politics, weather conditions and social issues. Delays in the construction environment are categorised into excusable delays, indicating that contractors were not at fault. They can be classified into non-excusable delays.

Non-excusable delays means the contractor has to take responsibility and compensate for the lost productivity time and is not eligible for compensation. The research also indicates that the construction delays may be concurrent or non-concurrent. The concurrent delays are considered to overlap. The non-concurrent delays do not occur simultaneously. Some of the delay causes recorded from previous construction projects, include amongst others (Amoatey and Ankrah, 2017:112):

- Changes to the designs.
- Weather conditions - extreme cold, hot or rainfall.
- Poor workmanship.
- Poor estimation of prices and shortages in material.
- Poor project management.
- Changes in site conditions.
- Late deliveries.
- A lack of supervision - mistakes during construction.
- The strikes and labour disputes.

- Poor coordination and scheduling (Amoatey and Ankrah, 2017).

The potential external risks hindering the project schedule, are mostly considered as uncontrollable. Amongst others, it includes technical, political, social, environmental and economic risks (Basak, Coffey and Perrons, 2017). According to the study, a schedule overrun may be defined as the inability or failure of the project to be completed within the pre-set dates and agreed timelines in the contract between the project stakeholders.

Basak, Coffey and Perrons (2017) investigated the risks in the natural gas projects, likely to cause delays and identified the damaging effects thereof in construction projects. Potential risks that could hinder the project performance were identified during the research to structure the risk management plan for the natural gas projects. The authors reiterated that it is important to identify project risks and their drivers. This will ensure that appropriate and prompt mitigation plans could be developed and implemented to manage the negative implications that risks pose in construction projects.

According to Basak, Coffey and Perrons (2017), the project risks could be categorised into external and internal risks and or nontechnical risks (NTR). They emanate from various sources. External risks contributing to project delays, emanate from social, political, economic, technological and legal factors. They cannot be controlled by the project team. They are driven by amendments to the Government laws and regulations, unstable political conditions, inflation, corruption, social issues, litigations and unfavourable weather conditions.

Sources of internal project risks are the client, contractors and consultants (Basak, Coffey and Perrons, 2017). The research revealed that internal risk drivers include design changes, slow decision-making, appointing in-experienced contractors, use of unreliable construction equipment, labour unrests, low labour productivity and rework, due to error in executions.

Some of the symptoms or signs most likely to be visible when a construction project is destined to failure include events, such as a project falling behind schedule. This suggests that tabling of a recovery plan to recover the lost time is required. This would likely indicate the deployment of more resources and unplanned overtime in the project, resulting in project budget depletion. Contract terminations, abandoning of projects, legal disputes and third party claims, often occur because of time-related matters in the project, such as late completion of projects (Islam *et al.*, 2014).

According to the study conducted in Saudi Arabia, 49 infrastructure projects were earmarked for the research to ascertain the root cause of project delays. Elawi, Algahtany and Kashiwagi (2016) shared that at least 70% of projects in this country are heavily affected by this widespread phenomenon of project delays. The methodology employed to conduct this study was qualitative. The study identified ten risk factors, contributing to the delay challenges. The following information represents the findings of the researchers from the 49 projects (Algahtany and Kashiwagi, 2016: 1403 - 1407):

- Ninety-seven per cent of delays occur at the completion stage of the project.
- Contractors were guilty of delaying 37% of projects.
- Serious delays were experienced on 84% of projects under mentorship of consultants.
- On average, project overruns were recorded to be in the range of 39% of the initial contractual set project duration.
- Research also indicates that project cost overruns were likely to affect 80% of projects.

Elawi, Algahtany and Kashiwagi (2016) investigated causes for delays in the Mecca province located in Western Saudi Arabia. The authors focussed on the bridge and rail projects, whereby they identified the responsible parties for delays in those construction projects in the province. The issue of land acquisition difficulties reached the top of the rankings as the most frequent risk factor to the project. Records indicate that rail and bridge projects were delayed on 15 occasions. Whilst the ranking table by Elawi, Algahtany and Kashiwagi (2016) indicates that the inexperience of the contractor contributes to 53% of delays, they recorded 12 cases. The study posits that all the project stakeholders (client, consultant and contractor) are responsible for delays in these road and rail projects. The external delay factors, such as politics and the economy indirectly cause these delays.

Malaysian construction was under scrutiny, whereby a study on construction project delays was performed. The following objectives of the study were identified:

- Ascertaining contributing factors to construction project delays, concerning finance or funding.
- Analysis of the stakeholders' reaction towards financial issues, causing delays.
- Mitigation and remedial actions to manage construction project delays.

Miller et al., (2017) revealed that the construction industry is one of the largest contributors to the economic growth of several global developing countries. This industry was identified to be influential concerning improving the quality of life and contributing to the growth of the GDP of several countries. In an article discussing financial issues, contributing to project delays (Abdul-Rahman *et al.,* 2009), it is mentioned that 110 participants from Malaysia took part in the study. Contractors, bankers, clients and consultants partook in the research. Some of their responses were recorded through questionnaire surveys, whilst others were captured during the scheduled interviews (Abdul-Rahman *et al.,* 2009). Figure 4 illustrates the linkage between dependent and independent variables.

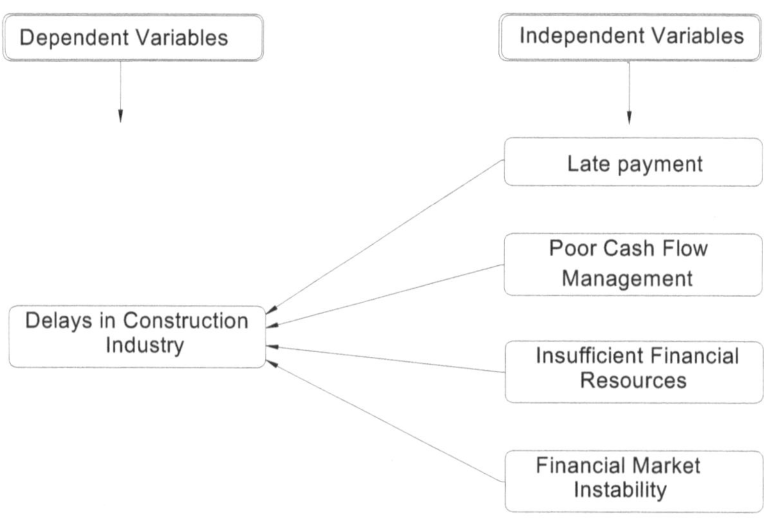

Figure 4: Relationship between Dependent and Independent Variables (Abdul-Rahman et al., 2009:230)

According to the revelations in the study, four main causes of delays in Malaysian projects are financially related. The concern regarding overdue payments is a serious challenge, confronting projects in Malaysia. The cash flow management is poor; lack of financial resources and the instability of the financial market were identified as major contributors to this costly problem, troubling the construction industry (Abdul-Rahman *et al.,* 2009).

If the project cash flow is poor, it is most likely that the construction delays may become greater. The remedial actions and plans to manage this problem according to the feedback from respondents, include the following (Abdul-Rahman *et al.,* 2009:235):

- The contractor should be paid timeously by the client.
- The advice to the client was to maintain a positive attitude and a well-managed cash flow, through business management education and improving their cash flow management skills.
- The banks were urged to accelerate the process in providing funds to qualifying clients.
- There was a call to amend the legislation regarding refunds and payments, to avoid ambiguity.

One of Ugandan major public enterprises, known as the Civil Aviation Authority (CAA) was the focus area in a research performed on a topic of causes of delays and cost overruns in construction projects in the Ugandan public sector. Several researchers in construction management (Ofori-Kuragu *et al.*, 2016), Doloi, Sawhney and Iyer, 2012) and (Abdul-Rahman *et al.,* 2009), revealed that the wealth of numerous developing countries globally, is directly influenced and dependent on their ability to upgrade and build new infrastructures through the construction industry.

Several global countries are confronted with this enduring challenge of project delays. Uganda also encountered massive delays and cost overruns in their public sector. According to Alinaitwe, Apolot and Tindiwensi (2013), an identified practical example of such a project was the Northern By-pass Kampala project. It is understood from the literature that the Kampala project exceeded the original estimated budget by over 100%. The project duration was beyond five years, whilst it was scheduled for two and a half years.

Developing an infrastructure is recognised as a crucial factor in stimulating economic growth of several developing countries; the challenges hindering the construction industry to deliver these projects timeously and within budget, have an adverse impact on this mission. Alinaitwe, Apolot and Tindiwensi (2013) state that during the 2011 to 2012 budget speech, it was envisioned that more than 45% of the Ugandan funds would be used on construction related activities. This undertaking identified Uganda as one of several developing countries. The country also strongly invests in the construction industry to grow its economy. The authors postulate that according to the records held by Uganda Bureau of Statistics (for the past few years), more than 12% of Ugandan GDP contributions was generated by the construction industry.

The questionnaire methodology was employed to collect the survey data from construction projects in Central Aviation Authority (CAA), which is one of the largest public enterprises in Uganda. The findings revealed that 46% of project delays are caused by alterations to the scope of work. Secondly, 21% of delays were due to delayed payments. Remote locations of projects caused delays by 15%, whilst 6% of delays were frequently caused by poor communication between the project stakeholders. Only 3% of project delays were due to the extreme weather conditions and disputes (Alinaitwe, Apolot and Tindiwensi, 2013).

It is recommended to minimising scope creeps, avoiding overdue payments to contractors and consultants and reduce overruns on cost and time. This would improve the delivery of infrastructure projects. It would also improve the efficiency and effectiveness in Uganda's public sector.

Alzara *et al.* (2016). publicised that Saudi Arabian construction projects were recently adversely affected by late completions and excessive budget depletion. According to Alzara *et al.* (2016), records indicate that 70% of the Saudi Arabian public projects suffer due to delays. The literature on this journal article focussed on the university situated in the Northern part of the country as the case study. The literature documented that the project endeavouring to build the university, commenced in 2006. It was scheduled to continue for six years. In 2012, the planned completion date, only two buildings were ready for use, whilst 22 more buildings were still under construction.

The objective of this study in Saudi Arabia, was to investigate root causes of delays in constructing the university and the impact thereof. The aim of the study was to compare the causes of delays from constructing the university with causes found in the majority of the country's public projects.

The study submits that 2330 projects were allocated a budget of over $48 billion by the minister of Finance in Saudi Arabia in 2013. Due to the project blockages and backlogs from 2013, the Government became uncertain and doubtful to further allocate $66 billion in 2014 as intended. The likelihood existed that the State would not gain value for their money and utility from those projects (Alzara *et al.,* 2016).

An interview with a stakeholder from the university was conducted to establish the views from the project owner's perspective concerning delay factors in the university construction project. Amongst other aspects derived from the interview, held on 14 and 15 March 2015, the interviewee observed the following: From twenty-two projects, seventeen experienced delays and eight were still in the design phase. The stakeholder in question, posited that project delays had an overrun time, ranging from 50% to 150%. Ninety-nine per cent of the university project costs exceeded the estimated costs. Some projects appeared to commenced construction with incomplete designs, suggesting that the university did not instigate proper planning.

Twenty-seven delay factors were identified in the South Arabian public projects through literature review. The university stakeholders also revealed twenty-seven delay factors, responsible for the university's construction delays. Subsequently, there was a comparison between delay factors revealed by the university and literature, regarding the country's public projects. Nine important delay factors were agreed on by the university and the literature. The study did not recognise the other delay factors as important. The table below indicates nine important delay factors identified in the study.

Alzara *et al.* (2016) conducted a study at the Case Study University (CSU) on the infrastructure development project, marred with delays for several years. The authors summarise the important delay factors and identify the project stakeholder concerned or responsible. According to Alzara *et al.* (2016:935), the contractor contributed to certain delays in the project because:

- The contractor did not hold sufficient capacity to execute the work (work force).
- The contractor was in-experienced.
- The contractor did not possess the necessary qualifications to perform the duties.
- The quality of the performance by the contractor was poor (inadequate).

The study revealed that the owner was guilty of delaying payments to contractors and time consuming reviews and approval of the designs (Alzara *et al.*, 2016). The bidding systems and procurement procedures were also identified as sources of delays; the authors did not identify the responsible parties.

Construction projects in India were subjected to criticism over the past few years. Development of a structural equation method was introduced into the fray to assist in the research of project delay causes. Recent studies identified the agricultural sector in India as the largest contributing sector to the country's GDP; the second largest contributor position is occupied by the construction industry with 6% to 9% annual GDP contributions (Doloi, Sawhney and Iyer, 2012).

The Indian construction industry has a lot to offer in growing the country economy. The construction sector though, are tainted with abandoned projects, delays, cost overruns and low productivity. A questionnaire survey was conducted, comprising 77 valid respondents. These included clients, contractors and consultants. The study identified four major factors that caused project delays that marred the Indian construction sector.

Poor planning is one of the contributors to project delays. Poor planning includes, a lack of communication between stakeholders, failure to cater for unfavourable weather conditions and failure to utilise equipment efficiently (Doloi, Sawhney and Iyer, 2012). Appointments of incompetent contractors were marred with unsatisfactory labour productivity, improper estimates and inabilities to manage the subcontractors.

The study reflected on the owner as a major contributing factor. Doloi, Sawhney and Iyer (2012) mention that contractors are often delayed because the owners do not avail themselves timeously to approve the designs and the work. The study conclude, mentioning that changes and additions to the project scope (known in the construction industry as "scope creeps") and execution errors leading to rework, contributed to schedule and cost overruns in construction projects.

Cost overruns and prolonged durations are enduring challenges in construction projects in Iran. This forms the basis that prompted a study to be conducted in this sector, investigating the causes. Iran is one of the developing countries in the Middle East. Their construction industry is one of the pillars and driving forces behind the economic growth in this part of the world. Latterly Iran comprehended projects with massive potential profits. Projections indicated, spinning from control and turning into exorbitant, costly, unprofitable and money losing projects because of delays in construction projects (Samarghandi *et al.,* 2016).

According to this study, delays in a construction project may be defined as the extension of the project duration. This definition contradicts the pre-set project plan, due to unforeseen circumstances. The objective of the study was to identify delays and to determine the reasons for delays. The study aimed to evaluate the probability of occurrence and to propose remedial actions. These may be employed to manage delays and promote risk management initiatives. This can be achieved by generating regression models. These models would allow project managers to measure the project costs and schedules for future projects, based on the delay profiles on Iran projects (Samarghandi *et al.,* 2016).

The data collection method for this research was divided into two sections: One section focussed on identifying delay factors. The other section was attentive to determining the probability of the occurrence of each delay factor (Samarghandi *et al.,* 2016). The project stakeholders, including the clients, consultants, regulatory bodies, contractors, industry experts and project managers, amongst others, were interviewed in an effort to ensure correct and accurate capturing of project delay factors. Results from respondents were comprehensively deliberated, and comparisons were made amongst similar studies.

The study alluded that the government-funded projects in Iran are governed by complex regulations concerning approval processes and the execution of projects. For example, conventionally, selecting contractors in Government projects was solely influenced by the bidder's price. Samarghandi *et al.* (2016) suggested that the challenge with that approach, is that low bidding does not guarantee that the successful candidate holds the technical ability to do the work.

Another identified challenge was the occasional lack of knowledge concerning the regulations, due to ignorance. Ambiguity was another factor causing confusion. Consequently, misinterpretations of the regulations and terminologies in the contracts caused costly legal disputes between clients, consultants and (Samarghandi *et al.,* 2016). The contractors' loyalty to outdated construction methods and a lack of attention to inflation were also identified as contributing factors to project delays. Pricing and cost construction methods reflected to be inaccurate.

The majority of foremost projects in Iran receive funding from Government and undergo Government processes, such as the budget approval discussion held in parliament. Political interference often tends to hinder smooth and timeous budget approvals. Procurement processes are often prolonged. Risk management plans and proactive planning is of utmost important to endeavour avoiding delays.

The industry experts signified the cornerstone of the research, predominantly involving the perspective of the construction industry professionals on causes of delays within the industry in question. According to Agyekum-Mensah and Knight (2017), recent empirical studies focussed on identifying causes of project delays, their frequent occurrences and their rankings, from data obtained from the respondents. The study focussed on establishing the viewpoint of the experts in the construction industry. This area of study was neglected during the past few decades.

Agyekum-Mensah and Knight (2017) postulate that globally, 40% of projects suffer from construction delays. This has adverse effects in the construction sector. Studies indicate that the United Kingdom (UK) is also severely affected by this widespread phenomenon, whereby 70% of projects experience schedule and cost overruns. Agyekum-Mensah and Knight (2017) state that a project delay is the "inability to meet the scheduled time". Figure 5 indicates the processes of Government-funded projects.

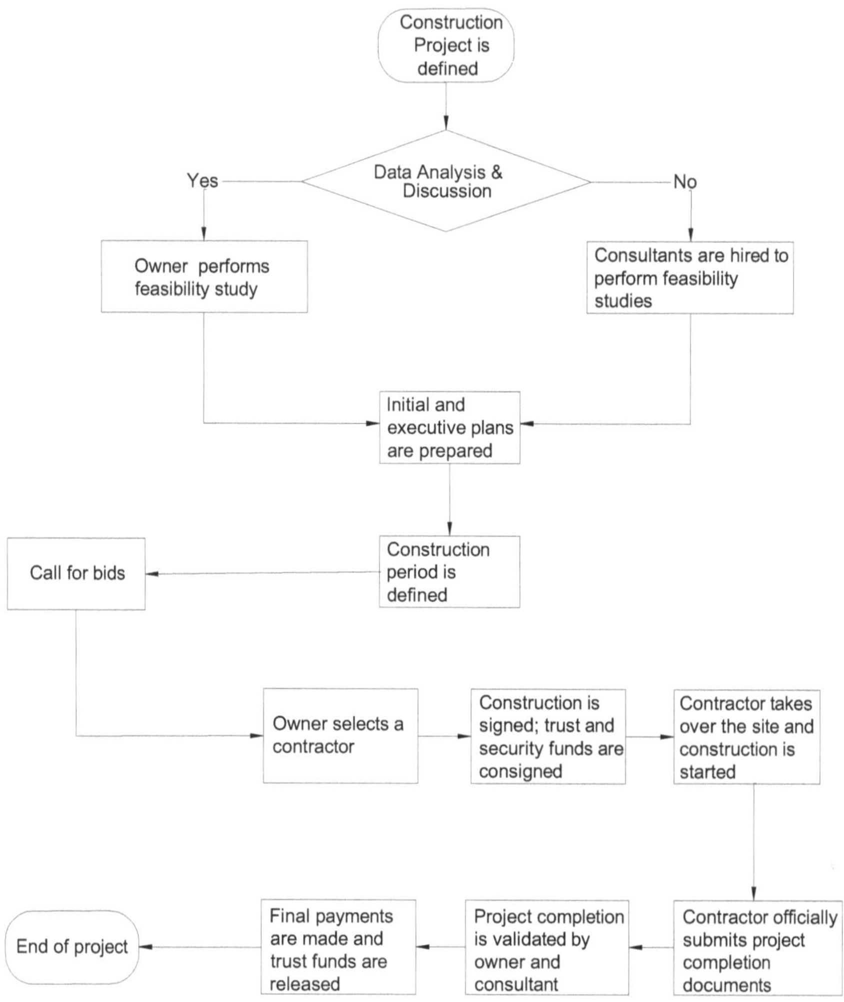

Figure 5: High Level Overview of Governmentally Funded Construction Projects in Iran (Samarghandi et al., 2016:68)

Agyekum-Mensah and Knight (2017) mentioned top 15 causes of delay as observed in construction literature. Table 1 below shows the causes of delays in the construction industry.

Table 1: Top 15 Causes of Delay Observed in Construction Literature (Agyekum-Mensah and Knight 2017:830)

Item	Common causes of delay	Raking based on occurrences
1	Poor planning	1
2	Commercial problems	2
3	Prolonged approval process	3
4	Changes to the scope	3
5	Unfavourable site conditions	4
6	Poor labour productivity	5
7	Changes to the designs	5
8	Insufficient material supply	5
9	Long lead items	5
10	Lack of site supervision	5
11	Extreme weather conditions	6
12	Fluctuation	6
13	Execution errors	6
14	Inexperienced contractor	6
15	Emergencies	6

Top 15 of delays were identified from the existing literature. Industry experts were interviewed to establish their viewpoint on project delays within the construction industry. The professionals' perspective and the findings of the case studies conducted on delay causes on construction projects were compared. Comparisons were made between the findings from the UK construction industry to the top 15 delay causes, ranked in the literature, as presented in the table above.

Pakistan (comparable to several other global countries) experienced delays in construction projects. This general phenomenon appear to be a recurring problem, leading to adverse effects in the construction sector. Studies revealed that project delays hold negative cost implications, adverse impacts on the project schedule, results in litigations, time extensions and arbitrations (Gardezi, Manarvi and Gardezi, 2014).

The study of time extension factors in the Pakistan construction sector, focussed on engaging contractors, clients and consultants to investigate the cause for the extension of time in the country's construction projects. The methodology that was employed to collect data, indicate consulting the database of the country's top companies or organisations. Fifty active projects (from the database) formed the basis of the study. Their reports, financial statements and other pertinent factors were considered. A questionnaire survey was conducted, and respondents comprised, the consultants, contractors and clients.

The College of DuPage (COD) in Illinois in the United States of America embarked on a project to revamp their campus, constructing a "state of the art" facility. The aim was to increase the student intake and ensure smart use of space (Dickson and Whitehurst, 2016). From the commencement of the project, the study reveals that the construction management team were involved to provide input during the design stage. The constructability experts made valuable contributions to the construction design, advising whether a particular design would be feasible to be implemented or constructed.

Dickson and Whitehurst (2016) stated that the crucial approach for this project was to include all the project stakeholders from the onset to avoid delays during the construction stage. The COD relied on the experience of the construction management team to advise on matters such as, ordering of materials and identifying long lead items. The fundamental principle embodied by the COD, is that planning is crucial in a project. They (COD) are of the notion that if "the whole team knows 'why?' behind the planning and design process, the result is an improved 'what?'" (Dickson and Whitehurst 2016). This approach yielded good project results, ensuring successful completion of the project. The project resulted in reduced operating cost of the renovated building, good-looking aesthetics and a state of the art facility.

Das and Emuze (2017) conducted a research on delay-causing factors in the context of construction projects in India. The findings of the research ascertained that in-experienced contractors often attend to rework because of errors during construction. Inadequate planning by the contractor was noted. India construction projects are marred with communication challenges amongst the project stakeholders, particularly the owner, the consultant and the contractor (Das and Emuze, 2017).

According to Das and Emuze (2017), the client often failed to reward the contractor with incentives on contract completion, accomplished prior to the set project schedule timelines. Another challenge in India projects, is the contractors' failure to manage the project financing, employing inappropriate construction methods and poor site management (Das and Emuze, 2017). This leads to possibilities for the occurrence of accidents and rework, translating into project delays.

Figure 6 illustrates and depicts the factors leading to rework in construction projects, subsequently delaying the project completion.

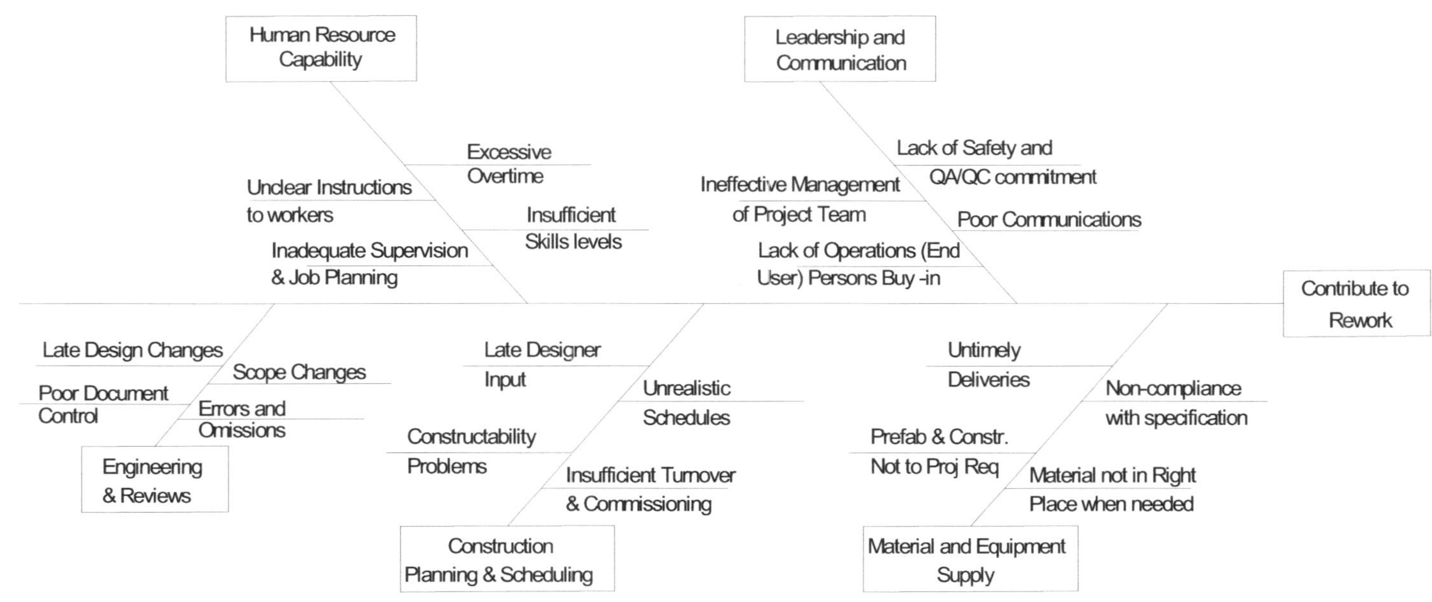

Figure 6: Rework Cause Classification Used in the Pilot Study (Aminah, Manjula and Oswaldo, 2004:1080)

2.5   Recommended Mitigation Measures

Risk assessment performed prior to the commencement of the project, is one of the crucial recommendations that needs to be implemented in the construction industry. Internal and external project risks have to be examined and predicted, ensuring thorough project planning. Stoudt (2013) states that programme management is the best instrument assisting cost reduction, improve efficiency and manage delays, hindering construction projects. Unlike construction management dealing construction phase issues in projects, programme management provides a holistic management in a project, from engineering design, procurement processes, construction phase, project funds, project timelines and project commissioning.

Bastianelli *et al.* (2012) proposed strategies for the successful running of construction projects, wherein the Front End Loading approach to capital projects was unpacked. Certain projects are simple and may be completed in a short period, without any difficulties. Certain projects are complex with a long duration. Some causes of complexity in projects often include issues of funding from Government, often marred by political interference, multidisciplinary interface and the size of projects, amongst others. Williams (2016) identified success factors in construction project through a cast study and Stoudt (2013) proposed the following twelve strategies that can yield success for construction or capital projects:

- Assessing the feasibility of the project:

The project budget needs assessment to ensure that it will be sufficient to cover the project costs and allow for contingency. Physical constraints to projects have to be evaluated, such as environmental conditions, minimising project risks. This undertaking requires the construction of a business plan, securing project funding, recruiting crucial personnel and engaging all the project stakeholders

- Define the project objective before commencement:

The scope of work of the project has to be clear from the onset; there should be no ambiguity. Liaise with all the stakeholders to ensure smooth approval processes for funding and engineering designs.

- Determine the duration and budget of the project:

It is crucial to know the estimated cost of the project and to be in a position to counter inflation risks and to ensure allowance for sufficient contingency. Similarly, establishing the estimated project duration, assists to plan and generate the project activity schedule.

- Securing of permits:

Safety campaigns are becoming prevalent in construction projects, encouraging safety to receive priority. Timeous application for necessary permits is of utmost importance and ensures compliance with the safety rules and regulations.

- Appoint qualified personnel:

Employing a team of professionals, improves the quality of work and promotes good engineering ethics and quality workmanship.

Ensure that the planning and engineering teams experienced working on a similar project to the planned project:

An experienced team who already know the operation of the system tend to accelerate the project because they know what is expected concerning compliance engineering regulations and best safety practices and the duration of each activity.

- Understanding of laws, rules and regulations that could hinder the project:

Having extensive knowledge in this area of expertise saves time and money, ensuring delivery of successful projects.

- Minimise incremental programme requirements:

Take cognisance and use volumes and market realisations as a guide during the project, to plan for future growth.

- Base size on a conservative business plan.
- Set achievable market share targets by developing a feasible and a balanced financial plan. The plan has to interface the operations, facility concepts and finance strategy.
- Evaluate the cost impact of the building footprint.

It is crucial to ensure that design verifications occur prior to generating the bill of quantities, ensuring that the estimated project costs are correct, avoiding miscalculations.

- Balance the cost and benefit of shelled space:

It is important for the project stakeholders to consider the possibility of future expansions and make provisions. There has to be a balance in the budget allocation; benefits needs to be considered carefully.

- Consider alternative delivery methods:

Source reliable service providers and check constantly on the placed orders to minimise last minute excuses, prior to delivery by the service provider. Subsequently, this could delay the project. Previous studies reiterate the significance of treating each project individually, and the dangers of using information of previous projects, similar to the project undertaken. Often this leads to a lack of attention to detail, leading to errors.

Project planning is one of the most crucial functions of project management. Early planning for a project is a strategy with the potential to accelerate the project and ensure timeous project completion. It is of utmost importance to encourage all the project stakeholders to partake during the planning phase; this assist project managers to foresee possible risks, allowing them to be proactive and plan better.

The discussions likely to take place during the project planning phase, include amongst others, the procurement of materials, to ascertain if the project requires long lead items and if they could be procured locally. Careful planning to recruit labourers is an important aspect to attend to during these engagements. This will avoid protests from local communities, especially in the remote areas. Delivery of materials and crucial project equipment has to be planned to align with the construction schedule, ensuring that the construction team will be ready to install the equipment immediately when the delivery is made to the site (Rentschler, 2017).

Cost overruns continue to be an enduring challenge for construction projects and persist to hinder their progress. Allowing for contingency when generating project estimates during the planning stage, is a measure that could be established to manage this problem. Contingency offers flexibility to the project manager, concerning finances. It provides for unforeseen circumstances with negative cost implications to the project.

Zakaria *et al.* (2017), Duke (2015) and Chan (2004) discussed critical success factors in construction projects and mentioned seven crucial elements for a successful completion of a construction project. These elements are discussed briefly as follows:

- Alignment of capital projects with the strategic plan:

The project needs to be part of the strategic planning of the business. It is the responsibility of the leadership team to identify such projects and ensure that they are prioritised in the pecking order.

- To realise that benchmarking is an art:

To run a successful project, benchmarking needs to be established and implemented, enduring proper conceptual cost development processes.

- Avoid premature launching:

It is advisable for the project team to fully understand the project scope and expected deliverables, prior to commencement of the construction, avoiding rework and unmet expectations.

- Develop team selection processes:

Appointing experience and reputable contractors (staff) for construction work in capital projects will expedite and promote an injury free project. This requires developing a team selection process or selection criteria.

- Communicate across party lines:

Top management needs to engage with all the workers, including those at the bottom of the organogram or hierarchy, ensuring communicating the strategic plans of the business to all involved (Duke, 2015).

- Create team accountability for the budget, scope and schedule:

Sharing of information between the project team members and creating an environment that makes sense to everyone, ensuring that their contribution in the project is meaningful, results in self-motivated individuals who tend to be creative and responsible in their work.

- Plan for the commissioning or close-out of the project, in advance:

During the conclusion of the capital project, the infrastructure has to be ready for occupation or use. Maintenance plans need to be in place. As-built data packs have to be submitted to the asset owner (Duke, 2015).

According to Swinson *et al.* (2016), employing project management instruments and techniques, could ensure successful completion of projects, regardless the size of the project. Good planning identifies crucial aspects, ensuring project success. The study reveals that the project is more workable and easier for the project team to expedite by divide the project into smaller parts, understanding the scope of work fully. Project planning assists in identifying tasks to be performed in parallel and those that are supposed to occur prior to the time; these are called pre-requisite tasks (Swinson *et al.*, 2016).

2.6 Studies Conducted in the Field

Table 2: Tabulation of Literature Review Findings

Researchers/Citation	Causes/Impact of delays	Respective proposed mitigation measures
Ansah and Sorooshian (2018).	External delays originating from sources outside the project and are beyond the control of the PM.	• The project team has to be circumspect and cautious with regards to the environmental factors.
Yang and Wei (2010)	The unceasing changes to the project developer's requirements.	• Warrants further research
Hussain, *et al.,* (2017)	• Mismanagement of funds by the contractor • Progress payment not paid timeously • Difficulties with site access • Incomplete feasibility studies • Focussing on low bid when awarding the project • Unfavourable weather conditions • Inadequate contractor experience • Incomplete survey and collection of insufficient data	• The financial standing of the potential contractor has to be reviewed and assessed prior to contract award. • Monitoring of construction progress on weekly basis. • All project designs has to be approved and re-checked against the scope of works. • Realistic and workable construction schedule to be submitted by the contractor. • Procurement of the servitude to be completed prior to project commencement.
(Sweis, Sweis *et al.* 2008)	• Poor planning by both the contractor and client. • Jordanian construction industry identified weather as the main cause of delays.	• No recommendations provided.

Researchers/Citation	Causes/Impact of delays	Respective proposed mitigation measures
Yang, Chu *et al.* (2013)	• Poor site monitoring • Amendments to Government laws • Client unavailability for inspection and acceptance • Opposition from the public • Scope changes	• Proactive planning and timeous identification of potential delay risks. • Recommended for further research, establish ways to minimise occurrences.
Rentschler *et al.* (2017)	• Low productivity • Squeezed schedules • Outsourcing, shortage of qualified stuff • Non-compliance to regulations • Complex contracts agreement or arrangements and adoption of new technologies	• Timely project planning is encouraged • Run independent construction activities in parallel • Allow for contingency • Involve construction team in the engineering processes such as designs • Organise labourers accordingly
Stoudt (2013)	• Environmental constraints • Approval processes • Difficulty to secure permits • In-experienced contractors • Lack of understanding of regulations	• Ensure that the planning and engineering teams has worked on a similar project previously with the one being undertaken • Minimise incremental programme requirements
Stoudt (2013)		• Understanding of laws, rules and regulations that could hinder the project • Explore alternative methods for deliveries

Researchers/Citation	Causes/Impact of delays	Respective proposed mitigation measures
Srdic and Selih (2015)	• Lengthy decision-making duration by client • Poor engineering deliverables • Failure to conduct project risk assessment	• No recommended mitigations provided
Amoatey and Ankrah (2017)	• Payment difficulties.	• Ensure availability of project funding prior to construction commencement.
Elawi, Algahtany and Kashiwagi (2016)	• The acquisition of land. • Design changes.	• Future research is recommended.
Doloi, Sawhney *et al.* (2012)	• Lack of stakeholders' commitment • Unqualified contractors	• PM to ensure there is alignment with project role players.
Chanmeka, Thomas *et al.* (2012)	• Commencing construction without complete engineering studies and designs	• Best project management practices to be implemented at an accelerated rate, such as conducting risk assessments
Parsons (2015)	• Incapacitated contractors accept more projects • Hiring of in-experienced contractors and consultants • Unrealistic designs by the engineering team • Political interference • Extreme weather conditions • Appointing a contractor because of the lowest bid	• Appoint experienced and reputable contractors and consultants. • Do not appoint a contractor based on the lowest bid price only. • More involvement of engineering team is recommended in projects to ensure complete and quality designs.
Zidane and Andersen	• Engineering design issues such	• Make IT services more

Researchers/Citation	Causes/Impact of delays	Respective proposed mitigation measures
(2018)	as software's technical glitches, such as Auto-cad licences • Design changes during construction • Improper and unrealistic designs	accessible, such as more office based IT Technicians • Promote good engineering ethics and accountability
Zidane and Andersen (2018)	• Shortage of project resources • Unrealistic project schedule and poor planning.	• Keep to the set milestones and crucial dates.
Lo, Fung *et al.* (2006)	• Improper planning • Squeezed construction schedule.	• Prepare a detailed construction plan.

Table 3 below summarises delay factors, identified by various researchers.

Table 3: Summary of Delay Factors

Delay-causing factor	Author/s
1. Scope changes	• Yang and Wei (2010) • Yang, Chu *et al.* (2013) • Chanmeka, Thomas *et al.* (2012)
2. Design changes during construction	• Elawi, Algahtany and Kashiwagi (2016) • Chanmeka, Thomas *et al.* (2012) • Parsons (2015) • Zidane and Andersen (2018)
3. Unavailability of the client for supervision/oversight/approval	• Yang, Chu *et al.* (2013) • Srdic and Selih (2015) • Doloi, Sawhney *et al.* (2012)

4. Shortage of project resources	• Zidane and Andersen (2018) • Parsons (2015)
5. Squeezed construction schedule	• Rentschler *et al.* (2017) • Zidane and Andersen (2018)
5. External interference, such as politics and weather	• Ansah and Sorooshian (2018) • Hussain *et al.* (2017) • Yang, Chu *et al.* (2013) • Stoudt (2013) • Parsons (2015)
6. Land acquisition	• Elawi, Algahtany and Kashiwagi (2016)
7. Payment difficulties	• Hussain *et al.* (2017) • Amoatey and Ankrah (2017)

2.7   Chapter Summary

The reviewed literature share factors that are acknowledged in project delays. These challenges experienced in construction projects, are global and they are costly. According to the literature reviewed, project delays result in project cost and schedule overruns, leading to project budget depletion and delays in the project.

Various authors researched the topic in question and most of them state that no level of planning can guarantee a project to be free of delays, regardless whether the project is small or large. In certain instances, project delays are caused by external factors beyond the project team's control. The consultant, client and contractor are responsible for project delays. The studies reveal that good relationships and communication amongst the project stakeholders could have a fruitful and positive impact on the project.

The iron triangle, comprising quality, time and cost, is often used in construction projects to assess the project's success. Several researchers indicate that the norm in the construction industry is that most parties consider the project more successful if it was completed ahead of schedule.

It is evident from the reviewed literature that numerous studies posit that it may not be possible to avoid delays completely; certain suitable mitigation actions could be implemented to manage delays.

Chapter 3
Research Methodology

3.1   Introduction

Chapter 3 aims to outline the research approach employed in this study. Qualitative and quantitative research techniques or methods are briefly explained. The chapter explains why the qualitative approach was considered suitable for this study. A 'mind map' for this research is added during the conclusion of this chapter.

The research approach is a deductive research. This chapter provides an explanation, clarifying why a deductive research approach was preferred to inductive research.

The literature reviewed in Chapter 2 and the research methodology in this chapter, form the basis for the conclusion, in answering the research questions.

3.2   Research Approach

A researcher should decide on the suitable research approach for the study, to provide a research direction and improve its efficiency. The researcher may decide to use a qualitative or a quantitative research method. Certain studies were conducted through the amalgamation of both qualitative and quantitative researches.

McCusker and Gunaydin (2015) mention that qualitative research focusses on understanding a particular pattern, behaviour or theory. The authors emphasise that qualitative research may be characterised by its methods, aiming to address questions such as "why?", "how?" or "what?".

A quantitative research's purpose is to answer questions, such as "how much or how many?" It involves measuring quantities under investigation (McCusker and Gunaydin, 2015). This study employed a deductive research approach and a quantitative research whereby the questions were answered deductively.

3.3   Research Design

This research were conducted through literature review and a questionnaire survey. The research endeavoured to conduct interviews, should the response rate on the questionnaire have been unsatisfactory, to provide the study with the necessary and credible primary data, analysed in Chapter 4.

Figure 7 depicts the research design block diagram.

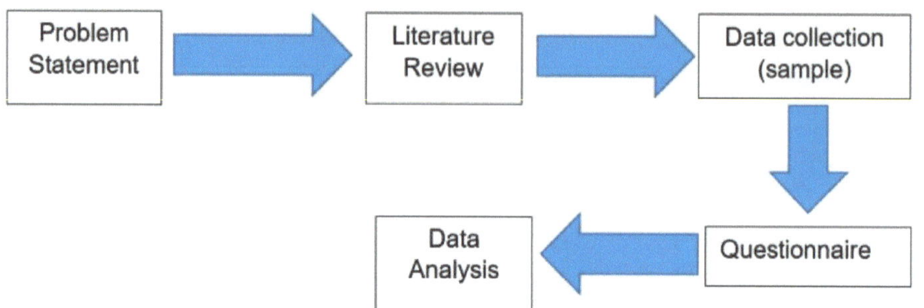

Figure 7: Research Design Block Diagram

3.3.1 Data Collection

For this research, both primary and secondary sources were used to collect the data needed to perform this study successfully. The purpose of the secondary data in this research was to collect information related to the focus area of this research, from information obtained from previous research. The secondary data offered an improved understanding of the topic and guided the structure of the questionnaire and the pertinent questions directed to the target population (Saunders, Lewis and Thornhill, 2012).

The primary data is referred to as the data or information collected from direct experience, indicating that it is a research field where the researcher interacts directly with the field experts (Saunders, Lewis and Thornhill, 2012). This may be achieved in the form of interviews with the individuals, based on the research field or area. It is useful to employ a primary data method to collect reliable and valid data (Saunders, Lewis and Thornhill, 2012).

Questionnaire survey method was employed to collect primary data. Collecting secondary data were conducted in a form of literature reviews from peer-reviewed journals, conference paper, reports and books.

Table 4: Primary and Secondary Research Methods (Skinner, 2010)

	Primary	Secondary
Definition	The researcher collects data from the original source first-hand.	It means the data that was collected by someone other than the researcher.
Sources	The primary source is an original document containing first-hand information about a topic	A secondary source interprets and analyses the information collected by the primary sources.
Source examples	<ul><li>Questionnaires</li><li>Interviews</li><li>Archives and manuscript material</li><li>Photographs, audio recordings, video recordings, films</li><li>Speeches</li></ul>	<ul><li>Dissertations</li><li>Journals</li><li>Articles</li><li>Newspapers</li><li>Internet</li><li>Published books</li></ul>

3.3.2 Sampling

Harrison and Mason (2008) referred to sampling as a procedure or a process used to select participants for a research from a particular target population. The study posited that in quantitative research, conclusions drawn by researchers, are often based on the general characteristics of a population that interests them.

It is not always practical to study the entire population due to the issues regarding cost implications, logistics and time constraints. The samples representing the target population, are often used to conduct the studies as they share the characteristics of a target population. Harrison and Mason (2008) indicate that the sample indicating the representing target population, needs to match their characteristics to ensure that correct data is captured and to avoid non-generalisation results.

Researchers use probability and non-probability sampling methods to determine the representative sample of a large group. Researchers use their own discretion or assumptions concerning the quantity of the characteristics that individuals share with the target population, to select participants for the survey during the non-probability survey. During the probability sampling, the selection of samples is random and unstructured (Harrison and Mason, 2008). Probability sampling offers individuals within the target population, an equal chance to be chosen to be part of the survey eliminating bias during the selection process as the selection is random.

The sample size has to be sufficiently relative to the target group, to boost it with adequate statistical power to detect a true influence and eliminate the possibility of incorrect conclusions.

- **Sample Space**

The focus for this research indicated the South African construction industry. The target areas were the construction sites in the Gauteng province, the Mpumalanga province and the KwaZulu-Natal province. Table 5 represents the geographical sample areas where the questionnaire survey were performed, including interviews when necessary. Several traction substation projects were proceeding and in the construction phase in these sample areas for Transnet and PRASA.

Table 5: Questionnaire Sample Areas

Province	City/Town	Municipality
Gauteng	Johannesburg	Johannesburg Metropolitan
Gauteng	Pretoria	Tshwane Metropolitan
KwaZulu-Natal	Richards Bay	uMhlathuze Local Municipality
Mpumalanga	Ermelo	Gert Sibande District Municipality
KwaZulu-Natal	Newcastle	Newcastle Local Municipality
Gauteng	Heidelberg	Lesedi Local Municipality

3.3.3 *Literature Review*

The literature review or desk research as alluded to by some authors, is covered in Chapter 2. The literature review involves analyses and a critical review of the published literature. It was pertinent to this research. The published literature reviewed to collect the necessary data required to perform this research, ranged from published peer-reviewed journals, books, articles, internet downloads, newspapers, online publications and correspondence.

The collected information formed the basis of the structure and the content of the questionnaire. It was supportive to conduct the literature review as it offered an improved understanding on the topic of causes of project delays in the construction industry. The reviewed literature answered some research questions and offered a global perspective on the issues concerning construction project delays.

3.3.4 *Questionnaire survey*

Leung (2001) mentions that a questionnaire is a popular research instrument used to collect primary data from individuals. The simplest questionnaires are unsurpassed and often yield more response from a large group of individuals, but the challenge is simplicity in a questionnaire.

The questionnaire could be designed to comprise open-ended and closed end questions. The closed end questions may be answered through dichotomous answers, Likert scales, semantic differential scales, importance scales or rating scales. Closed end questions could also be directed through multiple choices (Harrison and Mason, 2008).

The open-ended questionnaire is often unstructured, allowing the survey participants to answer questions in a manner that suit them best. The collected information tends to be an enormous quantity for the researcher to process accurately, within a short period; some of the responses tends to deviate from the original question (Harrison and Mason, 2008).

A questionnaire is a survey method used to collect information directly from individuals, relating to their preferences, personalities, level of understanding or attitudes. Questionnaires allow respondents to remain anonymous. Previous studies indicated that a questionnaire that is well designed, allows the same type of information to be collected from a significantly large number of individuals in the same manner (Fink, 2006).

Researchers aim to acquire information, pertinent to their research topic, when designing a questionnaire. The second objective in designing a questionnaire, is to obtain sufficient and maximised response rates (Leung, 2001).

A well-structured questionnaire uses simple sentences and directs precise questions. The researcher is cautious concerning sensitive issues, such as politics and race (Leung, 2001). Directing precise questions, one at a time, allows respondents to respond truthfully and correctly. Fink (2006:1-6) summarise the questionnaire into the following categories:

- Email or postal questionnaire - An individual completes a questionnaire, distributed as an email attachment or a postal mail.
- On the spot questionnaire - An individual completes a question 'on the spot' and presents it to the administrator.
- Web or internet based questionnaire - The questionnaire survey is conducted online whereby an email, or a link is shared with respondents.

The advantages and disadvantages of a questionnaire are as follows Fink (2006:1-6):

- Questionnaires are mainly directed after the event, as respondents are likely to forget important issues.
- The questions are usually short, therefore respondents who misinterpret the questions cannot be offered an explanation.
- Open-ended questions can lead to broad and ambiguous responses and the data to be processed may be too much to be processed in short period.
- Respondents tends to lose interest if the questionnaire is too long, answering superficially.
- Online surveys discriminate against individuals lacking reliable internet access.
- In certain instances, individuals complete pencil and paper surveys; the online survey might not yield expected results.
- Individuals with visual impairments or who cannot and read or write, are usually unable to partake in the survey (Milne, 2010).

Advantages of a questionnaire are discussed as follows (Milne, 2010):

- The feedback from respondents is more objective as the data collection approach is standardised.
- It is quicker to collect data through a questionnaire as a large number of individuals could participate at the same time, unlike the interviews where one or two individuals are interviewed at once.

- Unlike face-to-face interviews, a questionnaire is more comfortable for respondents, especially concerning sensitive matters.
- Online surveys can be completed anywhere and at any time (Milne, 2010).

The Likert scales to be employed in the questionnaire survey were as follows:

1   = Strongly Disagree (SD).

2   = Disagree (D).

3   = Neutral (N).

4   = Agree (A).

5   = Strongly Agree (SA).

The second Likert scales on the questionnaire were as follows:

1   = Never.

2   = Rarely.

3   = Occasionally.

3   = often.

5   = Always.

- **Questionnaire Design**

A questionnaire for this research comprises a set of questions, whereby the aim was to distribute them to the identified target population, indicating the population of field experts embarking on traction substation construction projects in the railway engineering industry. The questionnaire was distributed online, whereby an email were sent to the respondent; a questionnaire survey link was provided.

Every individual's response contributed to an improved understanding of the challenges of construction projects. All responses were of equal importance. It did not take longer than 15 minutes of the participants' time to complete this exercise.

The design of the questionnaire is such that the identity of respondents was kept anonymous. Respondents were not compelled to enter their names or contact details on the questionnaire, to protect their identity. An invitation was extended to respondents to contact the researcher and supervisor, whose contact details were displayed on the questionnaire should they wish to know the results of this research.

The set of questions in the questionnaire were submitted to the Ethics Committee of The Postgraduate School of Engineering Management in the Faculty of Engineering and Built Environment, at the University of Johannesburg (Bunting Road Campus). The committee's prerogative was to ensure that the research posed no harm or risk to the participants, and to assess the benefits of the research to the participant.

The committee reviewed the questionnaire to ensure demographics, such as participants' ages, religious beliefs, political affiliations amongst others, were treated with the required sensitivity. The committee questionnaire review eliminated any bias and discrimination concerning gender, race and religion.

The challenges this questionnaire aimed to conquered to be considered effective, include answering the following questions or concerns:

- Measurement errors - how valid and reliable is the questionnaire?
- Non-response error - will the generalisation of findings be at risk because of participants who did not respond?
- Sampling errors - how well is the representation of the target population concerning a sample?
- Selection errors - what is the probability of those selected?
- Frame errors - is the list from which the participants were extracted from, accurate?

Contents of a questionnaire:

The questionnaire structure comprised four main sections:

- Section A: Demographics - The participants' personal background data.

The first part of the questionnaire focussed on demographics, whereby general information, such as the participants discipline and working experience were requested.

- Section B: The project manager's role.

The second section of the questionnaire focussed on the manner in which construction projects are administered, paying special attention to the abilities of project managers. The objective of this section of the questionnaire was to understand the perception of respondents concerning project managers. This included issues such as: Do they think project managers needs to attend technical courses? Would they say that the technical training would improve the technical competency of project managers (especially newly appointed project managers)?

- Section C: Causes of project delays.

The third section of the questionnaire used a Likert scale of 1-5, whereby respondents had to answer how frequently they have encountered the project delay causes that were identified in the literature review in construction projects (traction substation projects) they were involved in.

- Section D: Recommended mitigations.

The participants were also required to provide an indication of the extent that they agree or disagree on the mitigations identified from the literature review; do they believe they would be suitable to manage project delays?

Validity and reliability:

Two tests are generally considered after collecting data, to check the effectiveness of a questionnaire. These tests are known as validity and reliability tests (Nkobane, 2012). It is possible for a questionnaire to be reliable but invalid, but a valid questionnaire is always reliable (Venkitachalam, 2015).

i.   Testing the validity of a questionnaire

Testing the validity of a questionnaire refers to testing the ability of a questionnaire to measure what is intended to be measured. According to Venkitachalam (2015), the validity test of a questionnaire refers to the ability of a questionnaire to measure what it is intended to be measured or to yield the required results. The main reasons why validity tests are conducted are stated as follows:

- It answers the question of whether the research investigation is addressing the questions it undertook.
- In addition, does it provide these answers by employing appropriate procedures and methods?

The validity testing is accomplished through the following means:

- Request the experts to assess the test.
- Experts compute the percentage of the relevant question.
- Thereafter take the average of all experts.

- If the value is greater than 90, then the questionnaire and results are regarded valid (Venkitachalam, 2015).

The questionnaire underwent the validation procedure whereby the Ethics Committee of The Postgraduate School of Engineering Management at the University of Johannesburg reviewed it. The Ethics Committee established that the questionnaire posed no harm or risk to the participants, and concurred that the research will benefit the participant. The questionnaire was deemed free from any bias and discrimination concerning gender, race and religion and was considered valid since it was relevant to the research topic.

Validity testing of the questionnaire offers the following advantages:

- Minimise ambiguities and bias.
- It promotes exceptional quality of data and credible information.

ii.   Testing the reliability of a questionnaire

Venkitachalam (2015) concluded that reliability testing of a questionnaire refers to establishing the questionnaire's ability to reproduce meaningful results. A questionnaire is considered reliable if the participants provide equivalent answers.

Reliability of a questionnaire is measured concerning:

- Stability - to ensure the equivalent results are acquired.
- Internal consistency - to ensure that the measuring instruments measure the same characteristic.
- Equivalence - it is employed if two observers measure a single phenomenon simultaneously (Venkitachalam, 2015).

4.1.1 Research Instruments

The following research instruments were identified and tabled below, indicating suitable tools to collect data for this study.

Table 6: Research Instruments

Research Instrument	Objective
Questionnaire	To collect data from project stakeholders, such as a contractor
Interviews	To collect data from project stakeholders, such as a contractor
Excel tool	To process the collected data

4.1.2 Target Population

The target group for this research encompassed the following stakeholders in PRASA and Transnet's substation construction projects:

Project managers, electrical engineers and technicians, civil engineer and technician, construction managers, quantity surveyors, architects, quality inspectors, cost engineers, SHE officers and planners.

The questionnaire was distributed 150 people via an online programme called QuestionPro. Eighty-three responses were recorded. The average time taken to complete the questionnaire was 12 minutes. None of the participants abandoned the process during participation. All the responses are valid as the online survey was instituted to hinder respondents to continue to the following question without answering the current or the previous question.

The questionnaires also targeted the same professionals from the contractor and consultant's teams respectively, rendering engineering and project management services to PRASA and Transnet.

4.2   Research Questions

The research questions are stated as follows:
- What are causes of delays in traction substation projects within railway engineering?
- What mitigation plans which could be implemented to manage project delays?

4.3   Research Methodology

Sources for this research indicate the following:
- Literature reviews.
- Questionnaire surveys.

- Interviews.

A related literature review is conducted on the topic in question, prior to commencing with the study, to gain a firm and meaningful theoretical understanding. This assists to identify and determine possible factors, causing delays in construction projects.

For this research, a questionnaire survey approach was preferred as it was more suitable. The questionnaire was designed to be anonymous, protecting individuals' identities. It was distributed to all the project stakeholders. Interviews were conducted with the willing parties. Nobody was forced to participate in the research against their will. The systematic research methodology for this study is structured as follows:

Step 1: The first step for this research was to conduct a literature review on the topic in question, establishing the perspective and viewpoints of theorist and researchers who previously conducted research on the topic. This literature review was used as a basis or benchmark and was compared with the field data acquired through a questionnaire survey.

Step 2: The questionnaire is designed with the aim of supporting and answering research questions. The questionnaire questions were derived from the reviewed literature. The draft questions are attached as appendices.

The questionnaire questions were compiled based on the summary from the literature review; the research comprises two research questions:

- What are the cause and the impact of delays in traction substation projects within railway engineering?
- What mitigation strategies could be implemented to manage project delays?

The distribution of the questionnaire indicated project role players, particularly those who spent sundry time on sites, such as project managers, project engineers and contractors.

The questionnaire was accompanied by a cover letter; the following information are included in the letter (Appendix 1):

- The purpose of the questionnaire survey.
- Explains the reason the recipient was chosen to take part in the survey.
- Explains the benefits for the respondent to participate in the survey.

Step 3: The determined sample area of this research was construction projects of traction substations in Gauteng, Mpumalanga and KwaZulu-Natal, for Transnet and

PRASA. The aim was to employ an online questionnaire survey. If the response rate was unsatisfactory, interviews would have been conducted to increase the primary data collection.

Step 4: Collected or received online feedback for the questionnaire; processed the data. The targeted survey response indicated 100 responses, declaring the questionnaire survey fruitful and successful.

Step 5: Compared the views, opinions, perspectives and substances of the arguments from the literature review and compared it with the data collected through a questionnaire survey.

Figure 8 illustrates the direction that enabled conduction of the research.

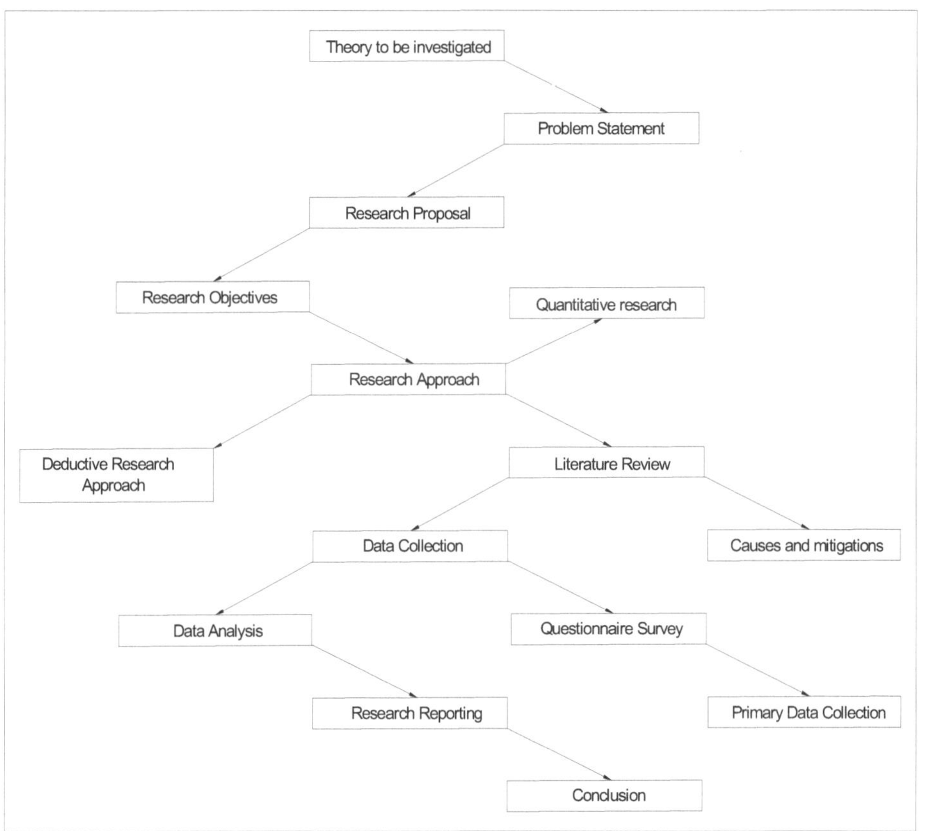

Figure 8: Research Mind Map

4.4 Delimitations

This research focussed within the South African construction industry. The target areas were the construction sites in the Gauteng province, the Mpumalanga province and the KwaZulu-Natal province. The area of interest for the research was project and construction management, establishing the influence, identifying the potential causes of project delays. The study also aimed to determine suitable remedial actions to be implemented.

Respondents in this research were the stakeholders, such as clients, suppliers, contractors, developers or engineers and construction workers (general workers, safety offers, construction managers and project managers).

4.5 Ethical Considerations

To ensure a credible outcome, it was of utmost importance that the researcher, collecting data, did not participate as a research subject. It is a moral and ethical obligation to ensure pure, truthful, reliable results that are unbiased.

The research held reliable ethical principles and high moral standards, indicating great respect for all participants. All participants were treated as anonymous agents. Individuals with diminished autonomy were entitled to protection; therefore, they were not forced to participate in this research.

4.6 Chapter Summary

The objective of Chapter 3 is to articulate the methodology employed in this research, to obtain all the necessary information. The contents of this chapter also states the data collection instruments and methods used in this study. The results of the survey are presented and analysed in Chapter 4.

Chapter 4

Data Presentation and Analysis

5.1   Introduction

This section presents the results of the questionnaire survey conducted for the research. The questionnaire was divided into the following sections:

- Section A: Demographics.
- Section B: Project management - (role of project managers).
- Section C: Causes of project delays.
- Section D: Recommended mitigations.

The questionnaire was distributed using an online programme called QuestionPro. Eighty-three responses were recorded. None of the participants abandoned the process during participation. All the responses are valid as the online survey was instituted to hinder respondents to continue to the following question without answering the current or the previous question.

The system prohibited submission at the end of the survey, should a question be unanswered during the process. The detailed survey results are available as appendices to this report. Figure 9 represents the questionnaire response rate.

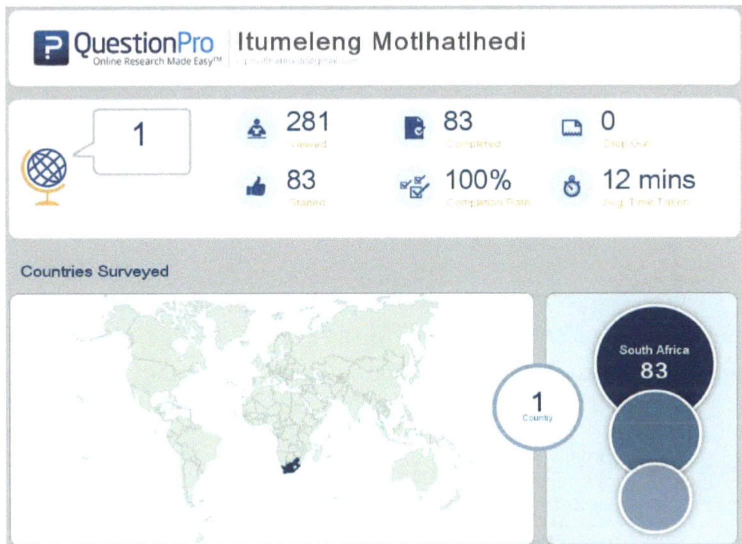

Figure 9: Online Survey Response Rate

5.2 Presentation and Analysis of Data

5.2.1 Section A: Demographics

The target group for this study was mainly the individuals with experience in construction projects, targeting traction substations. The employees from railway engineering companies (Transnet and PRASA) (including consultants and contractors) participated in the survey. Figure 10 indicates that 40 of the 83 respondents in the survey represented electrical engineers (48%). Civil engineers were presented with the second highest percentage, registering 20% on the chart, followed by project managers, indicating 7%.

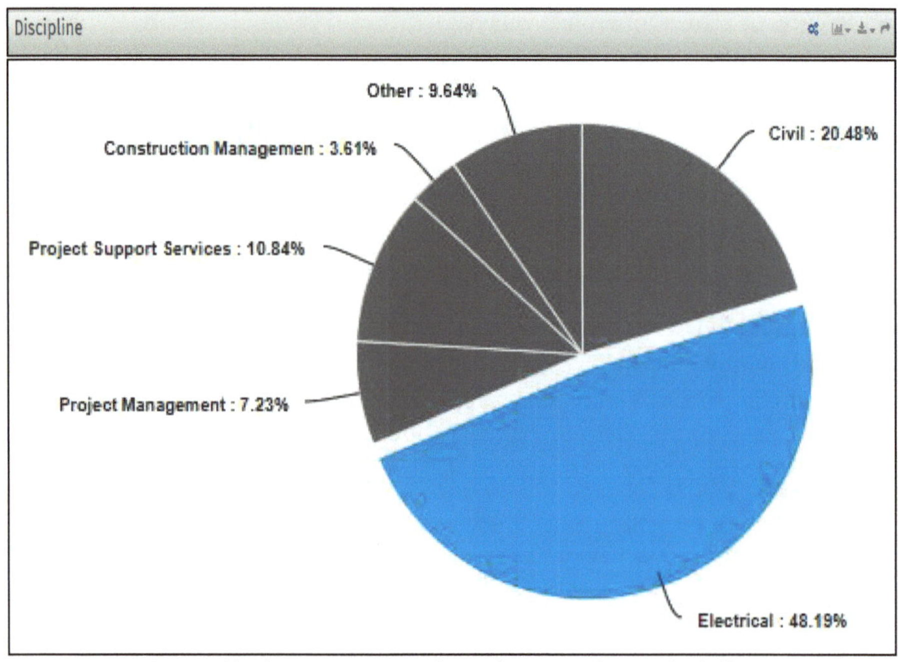

Figure 10: Survey Respondents from Various Disciplines

The questionnaire sample areas focussed on three provinces: Gauteng, Mpumalanga and KwaZulu-Natal. The survey results (figure 11) indicated Gauteng, presenting the highest number of respondents in the survey, particularly in Johannesburg Metropolitan with an 86% participation in the survey.

The feedback received, emphasised that the project team comprised individuals who hold low qualifications, such as matric. It also included those who hold highly ranked qualifications, such as a Masters Degree in Business Leadership (MBL), Masters Degree in Business Administration (MBA) and Project Management Professional

(PMP). This indicated variety concerning the skills applied, managing construction projects. See figure 12 below.

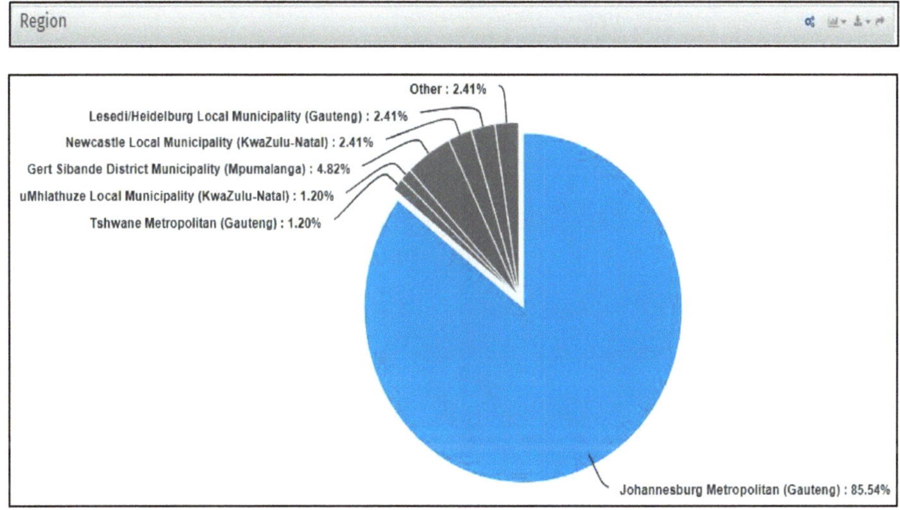

Figure 11: Survey Respondents from Various Regions

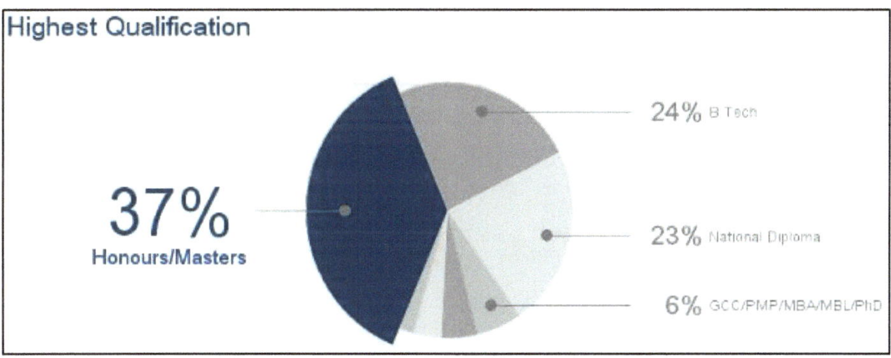

Figure 12: Survey Respondents' Qualifications

Figure 12 illustrates that project team members mostly hold Masters Degrees, B.Tech Degrees and National Diploma qualifications in various fields of studies. This includes, but is not limited to, electrical and civil engineering, and project management. Sixty per cent of construction projects of traction substations indicates electrical engineering. Civil engineering indicates 30% to 40% of construction projects. This explains electrical engineers' higher survey participation, opposed to participants from other disciplines.

The findings revealed that several individuals in the construction industry, particularly in railway engineering, are the youth. They are still capacitating themselves and gaining experience. Figure 12 illustrates that 37% of the construction project teams comprise individuals with less than five years' experience in the industry. Figure 12 indicates the results of the survey respondents' working experience within the project engineering environment.

Table 7: Survey Respondents' Field of Work

Answer	Count	Percent
Project Manager	9	10.84%
Electrical Engineer/ Technician	35	42.17%
Civil Engineer/ Technician	16	19.28%
Construction Manager	6	7.23%
Quantity Surveyor	0	0%
Architect	4	4.82%
Quality Inspector	3	3.61%
Cost Engineer	2	2.41%
SHE Officer	1	1.2%
Planner/Document Controller	5	6.02%
Other	2	2.41%
Total	**83**	**100 %**

Profession

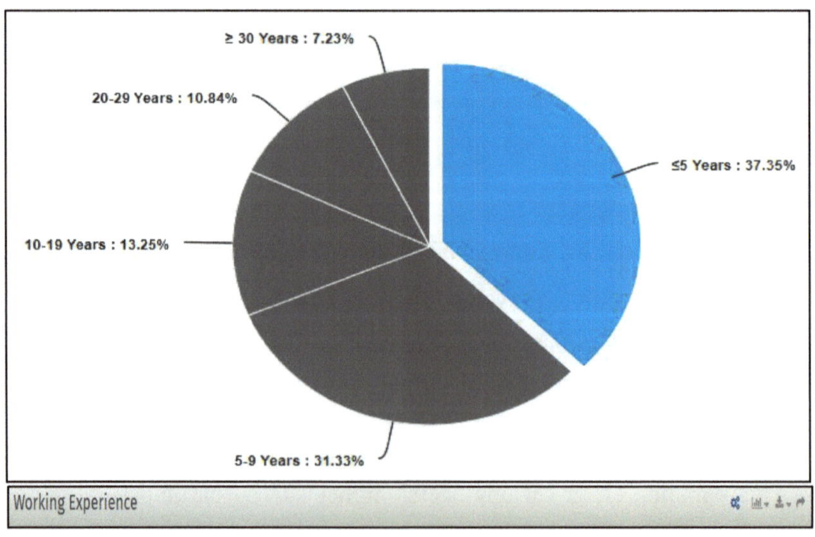

Figure 13: Survey Respondents' Work Experience

5.2.2 *Section B: The Role of Project Managers in Project Management*

The aim of this section was to establish the role for project managers in construction projects and whether they fulfil their duties. This section of the questionnaire focussed on the manner that construction projects are being administered, with emphasise on the capabilities and abilities of project managers. The objective of this section of the questionnaire is to understand the perception of respondents concerning project managers.

The factors of concern include: Do they sense that project managers need to attend technical courses? Do they believe that technical training would improve the technical competency of project managers (especially newly appointed project managers)? Figure 13 indicates the response statistics on Section B of the questionnaire, as signified by 13 to 15:

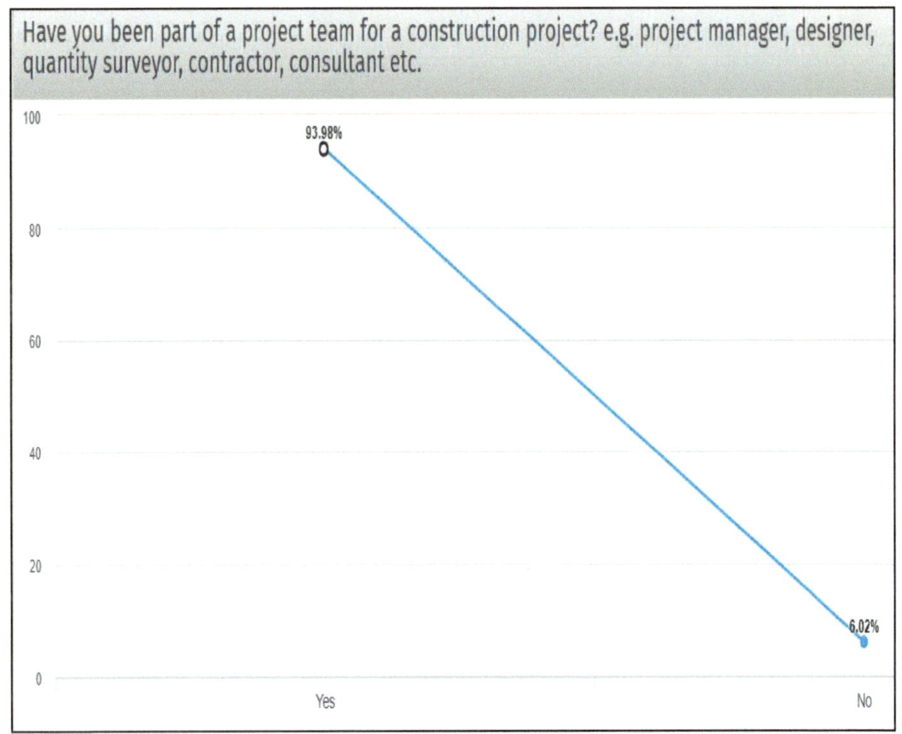

Figure 14: Survey Response to Section B

Figure 14 indicates results of Section B of the questionnaire.

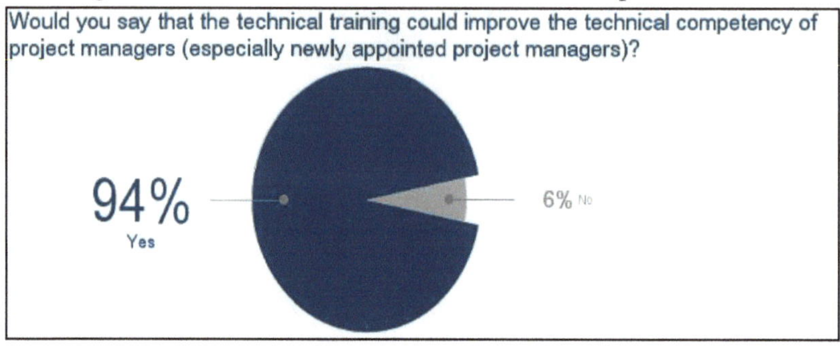

Figure 15: Survey Response to Section B

Respondents' feedback received (92%) believe that it would be in the best interest of the project if project managers attend technical courses. Respondents believe that if project managers could have an improved understanding of basic aspects, such as the project scope and milestone, it could minimise planning errors and irregularities. The participants signified that technical training would be of immense benefit to project managers, especially to in-experienced newly appointed project managers. Training would improve their technical competency.

The questionnaire findings signify that 81 of the 83 survey participants observed that proactive planning and timeous identification of delay risks are traits of a good project manager. Most respondents indicated that efficient project managers provide leeway and flexibility to their project team, applying their own methods when performing their duties. They should not dictate or micro-manage the team. Only 24% of the respondents indicated that project managers should monitor the project team closely, constantly reporting on their performance.

Figure 15 indicates results of Section B of the questionnaire.

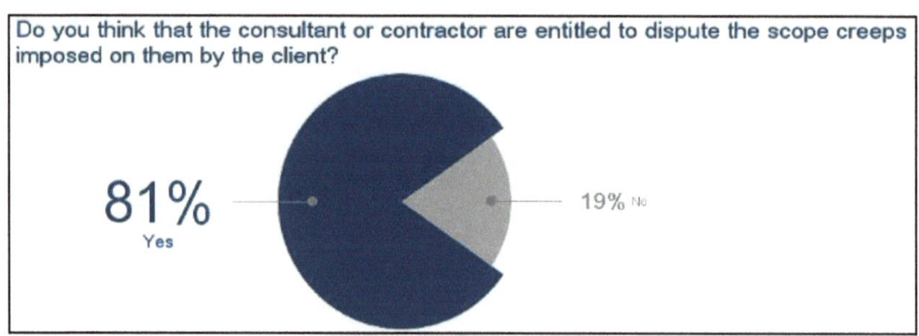

Figure 16: Survey Response to Section B

The survey results indicates that project manager's inability to work with the project team could lead to project failure. Sixty-nine of 83 respondents (83%) were negative towards the perception of project managers directing the project role players, dictating them on what methods to use, whilst performing their duties.

Table 8: Summary of Section B's Survey Responses

Question	Count	Score
Have you been part of a project team for a construction project? e.g. project manager, designer, quantity surveyor, contractor, consultant etc.	83	1.06
Do you think project managers needs to attend technical courses?	83	1.07
Would you say that the technical training could improve the technical competency of project managers (especially newly appointed project managers)?	83	1.06
Is proactive planning and timeous identification of potential delay risks one of the traits for a good project manager?	83	1.02
Do you think to expedite construction projects; it is advisable to run independent construction activities concurrently?	83	1.16
Does the client have a right to change the scope of work?	83	1.13
Do you think that the consultant or contractor are entitled to dispute the scope creeps imposed on them by the client?	83	1.19
Do you think a good project manager should micro-manage his/her project team?	83	1.76
Do you think that the project manager should be a dictator in order for the project to succeed?	83	1.83
Does the client have a right to change the scope work?	83	1.1
	Average	1.24

Questionnaire respondents expressed their disagreement on the client's rights to change the scope of work. Recorded results indicated that 81% of participants were of the notion that the consultants and contractors are entitled to dispute the scope creeps, imposed by the client.

The score in Table 8 indicates that the results can be interpreted according to the following ratings used:

- Yes = 1.
- No   = 2.

The scores in Table 8 indicate that "Yes" was the most general response to the questionnaires, hence the average questionnaire score recorded as 1.24.

5.2.3 Section C: Causes of Project Delays

The third section of the questionnaire used a Likert scale of 1-5, whereby respondents had to answer how frequently they encountered project delay causes in construction projects, identified in the literature review (traction substation projects). The responses are indicated in the figures below, from Figure 16 to 19.

The results indicated that scope changes are often experienced in construction projects. This could be because of factors, such as an indecisive client, technological changes, financial constraints amongst others (according to the literature review).

Over 40% of the feedback identified a setback in construction projects is caused by changes made to designs during construction phase of the project and this is experienced often. Only 6% of the participants indicated that they did not encounter delays, caused by design changes in their projects. Figure 18 indicates results of Section C of the questionnaire.

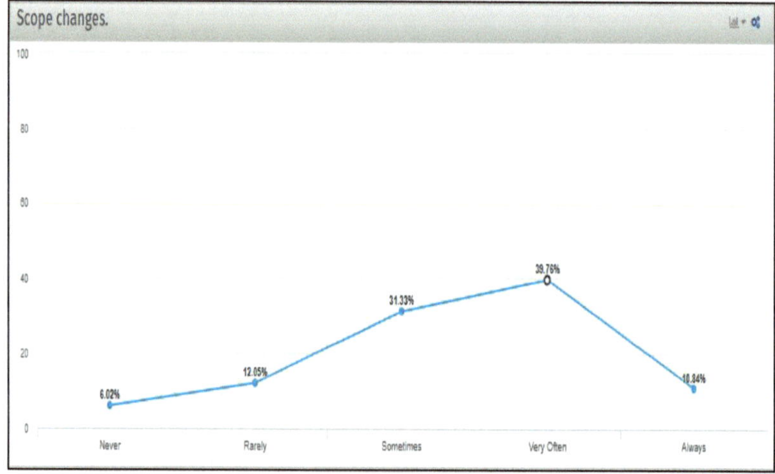

Figure 17: Survey Response to Section C

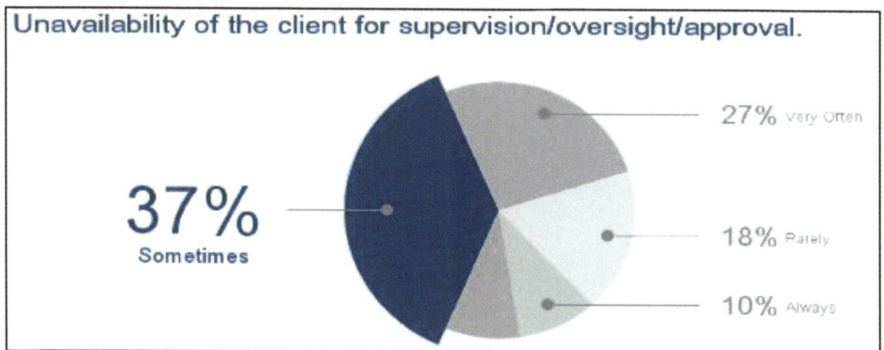

Figure 18: Survey Response to Section C

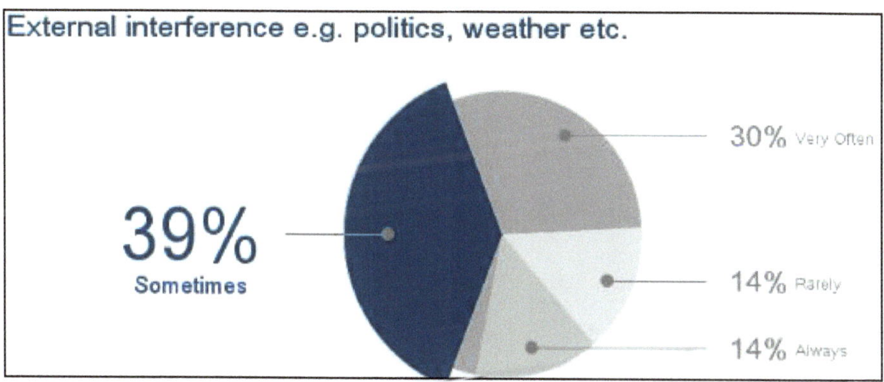

Figure 19: Survey Response to Section C

The results suggested that Transnet and PRASA are available frequently when client supervision, oversight and approval are required. Only 37% of respondents indicated that they occasionally encountered a situation where the client was unavailable when required on site. The situation caused delays in the project.

The collected data submitted that the survey participants sensed that resource shortages also contributed to project delays; 36% claimed experiencing resource shortages occasionally; 25% of respondents indicated that they experienced the resource shortages often in the duration of their projects.

Land acquisition from farmers and communities seems to indicate a minor challenge for traction substation projects, since several respondents (40%) indicated that they encountered related challenges in their projects occasionally but not often.

Te 9 indicates results of Section C of the questionnaire.

Table 9: Survey Response to Section C

Shortage of project resources.		
Answer	**Count**	**Percent**
Never	4	4.82%
Rarely	22	26.51%
Sometimes	30	36.14%
Very Often	21	25.3%
Always	6	7.23%
Total	**83**	**100 %**

The score in Table 9 indicates that the results can be interpreted according to the following ratings:

- Never   = 1
- Rarely   = 2
- Occasionally = 3
- Very Often = 4
- Always   = 5

The scores in Table 10 indicate that "Occasionally" and "Very Often" signified the most recorded responses from the survey participants, hence the average score of 3.11. Figure 20 below shows a summary of the results for section C of the questionnaire as recorded by the QuestionPro online survey programme.

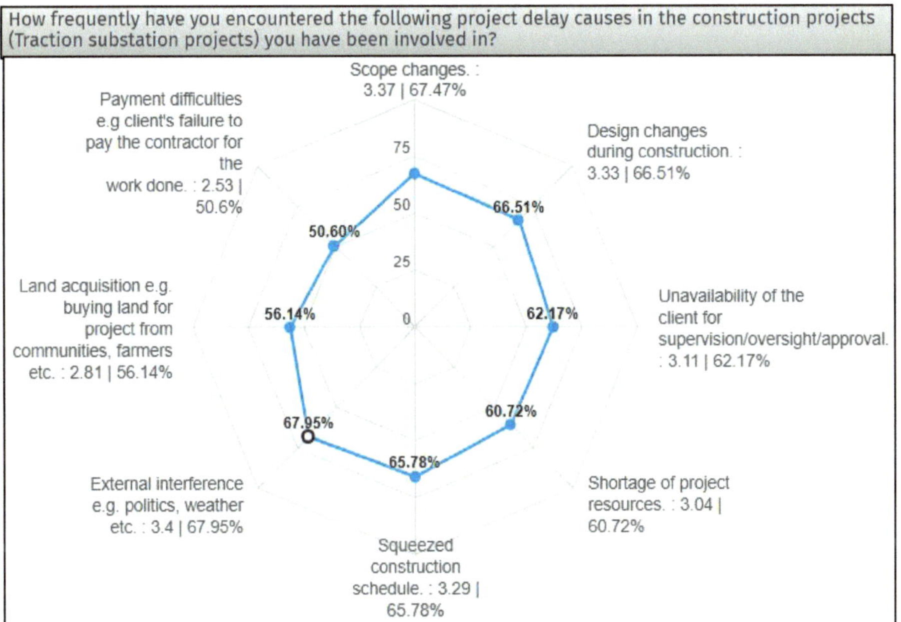

Figure 20: Summary of Section C's Survey Responses

Table 10: Summary of Section C's Survey Responses

Question	Count	Score
Scope changes.	83	3.37
Design changes during construction.	83	3.33
Unavailability of the client for supervision/oversight/approval.	83	3.11
Shortage of project resources.	83	3.04
Squeezed construction schedule.	83	3.29
External interference e.g. politics, weather etc.	83	3.4
Land acquisition e.g. buying land for project from communities, farmers etc.	83	2.81
Payment difficulties e.g client's failure to pay the contractor for the work done.	83	2.53
	Average	3.11

5.2.4 Section D: Recommended Mitigations

The participants were also required to indicate the extent that they agreed or disagreed with the mitigations, identified from the literature review. Their observations regarding those measures could be suitable to manage project delays.

Figures 21 to 26 indicate their responses measures could be suitable to manage project delays.

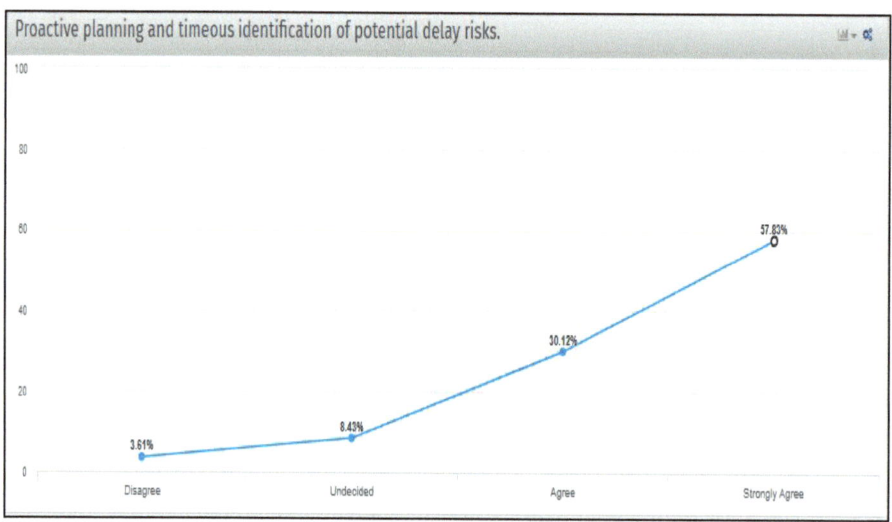

Figure 21, 22: Survey Response to Section D

A majority of 58% strongly agreed that proactive planning and timeous identification of risks in construction projects could be instrumental in minimising project delays. The captured results also indicated that only 4% of respondents disagreed, whilst 8% was undecided.

Forty-six respondents (from 83) agreed that independent project activities may be run parallel or simultaneously, to expedite the project's progress.

Figure 23 indicates results of Section D of the questionnaire.

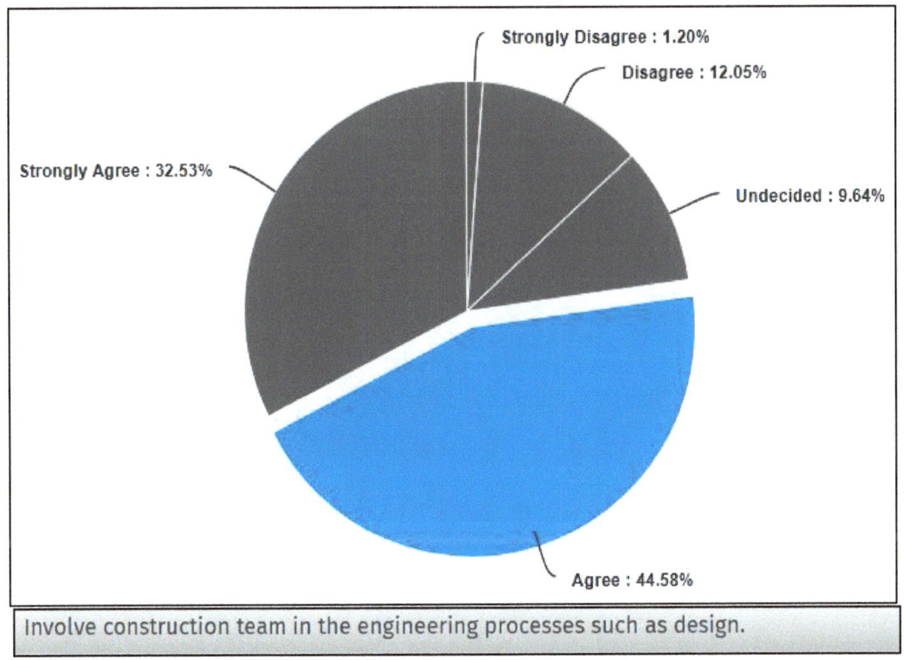

Figure 21: Survey Response to Section D

Respondents (46%) agreed that the designers should involve the construction team during the development of engineering designs. The principle is that this exercise benefit the project as the construction team were frequently on site. They are more familiar with the surroundings and temperatures. They could provide engineers with relevant information to be considered during the design phase.

Figure 24 indicates results from Section D of the questionnaire.

Answer	Count	Percent
Strongly Disagree	0	0%
Disagree	2	2.41%
Undecided	4	4.82%
Agree	38	45.78%
Strongly Agree	39	46.99%
Total	83	100 %

Figure 22: Survey Responses from Section D

According to 54% of respondents, it would be in the best interest of the project to ensure that the planning and engineering teams experienced a similar project to be knowledgeable on the planned assignment.

The survey results revealed that the participants' perception is that the construction projects' contractors should not be appointed, based solely on the lowest remuneration offered; 49 respondents (from 83) strongly agreed, and 17 participants agreed.

Figure 25 indicates results from Section D of the questionnaire.

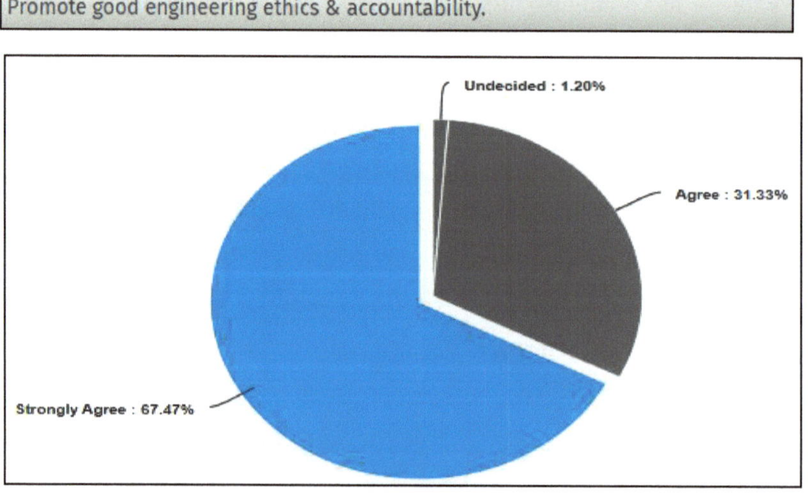

Figure 23: Survey Responses to Section D

According to figure 26, the results (47%) revealed respondents' observations is that understanding laws, rules and regulations, is crucial in managing project delays. A lack of understanding these aspects could hinder the project's progress. Appointing experienced contractors and consultants appeared to be welcomed by 90% of the participants; 47% agreed and 46% strongly disagreed.

Respondents mutually agreed to adhering to the set milestones and crucial dates. The majority of respondents agreed and strongly agreed to have this mitigation implemented to manage project delays.

Figure 26 indicates further results from Section D of the questionnaire.

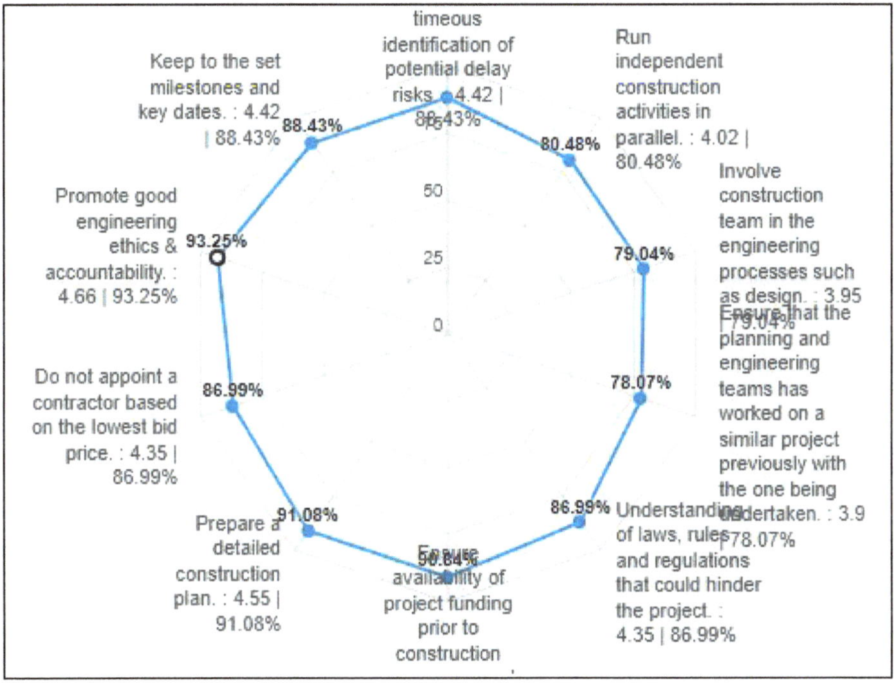

Figure 24: Alternative Survey Responses to Section D

The general perception is that effective engineering ethics and accountability need to be promoted. No objections to this recommended mitigation were indicated; 68% strongly agreed, 31% agreed and 1% was undecided.

Table 10: Summary of Section D's Survey Responses

Question	Count	Score
Proactive planning and timeous identification of potential delay risks.	83	4.42
Run independent construction activities in parallel.	83	4.02
Involve construction team in the engineering processes such as design.	83	3.95
Ensure that the planning and engineering teams has worked on a similar project previously with the one being undertaken.	83	3.9
Understanding of laws, rules and regulations that could hinder the project.	83	4.35
Ensure availability of project funding prior to construction commencement.	83	4.54
Prepare a detailed construction plan.	83	4.55
Appoint experienced and reputable contractors & consultants.	83	4.37
Do not appoint a contractor based on the lowest bid price.	83	4.35
Promote good engineering ethics & accountability.	83	4.66
Keep to the set milestones and key dates.	83	4.42
	Average	4.32

The scores in Table 10 indicate that the results can be interpreted according to the following ratings:

- Strongly disagree = 1
- Disagree = 2
- Undecided = 3
- Agree = 4
- Strongly agree = 5

The scores below indicate that most responses were "Agree" and "Disagree"; the average score is 4.32.

5.3   Chapter Summary

The targeted number of respondents for the questionnaire survey was 100. Eighty-three responses were received for two weeks. No 'dropouts' were indicated during the survey, as those who started the survey, continued until the conclusion and submitted their responses.

All the questions in the survey were answered. The average completion rate for the online survey was 12 minutes. All respondents were South Africans; the highest participation rate was from Johannesburg in the Gauteng province.

Electrical engineers recorded the highest response rate on the survey, followed by civil engineers. Most participants held less than five years' experience in the construction industry. Project engineering with the second highest participation, was from respondents with five to nine years working experience.

Chapter 5

Discussion of Findings

Chapter 5 interprets, analyses and discusses the findings and data presentation from Chapter 4. The questionnaire was designed with the aim of supporting and answering research questions. The questionnaire research questions were derived from the reviewed literature and the draft questions of the questionnaire.

5.1   Section A: Demographics

The questionnaire was distributed to the project role players, particularly those who spent a considerable time on the site, such as project managers, project engineers and contractors.

The determined sample area for this research was construction projects for Transnet and PRASA of traction substations in Gauteng, Mpumalanga and KwaZulu-Natal. The aim was to use an online questionnaire survey. If the response rate was considered unsatisfactory though, interviews would have been considered to increase the primary data collection.

The figure below indicates that 83 survey responses were received. This number was considered sufficient and satisfactory for the intended purpose. It was therefore unnecessary to conduct interviews.

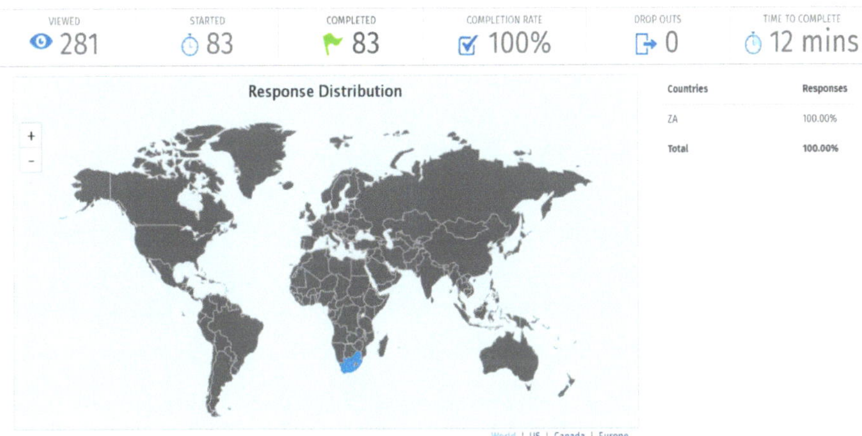

Figure 25: Questionnaire Survey Statistics

More than two thirds of the survey respondents were from the Gauteng province, suggesting that most of PRASA and Transnet traction substation projects are managed from Gauteng; 71 of the 83 responses received were from individuals, residing in the province (Gauteng).

The survey successfully received feedback from almost all the project role players to whom the questionnaire was distributed, with the exception of quantity surveyors who did not respond to the survey invitation. Construction managers, project planners, project managers, project engineers, consultants, SHE representatives, consultants and contractors honoured the invitation and participated in the online survey.

According to the survey results, approximately 42% of the responses were from electrical engineers, as approximately 60% to 70% of the operations on the traction substation projects involves electrical work mainly. Civil engineers also participated in the survey, recording 19%. The results revealed that other disciplines, such as architecture, chemical and finance participated, even though they were not the target group. It was a powerful addition because it provided new perspective from individuals not directly involved with projects of this nature.

The collected data suggested that the youth are the helm of these construction projects, since 37% of respondents had less than five years of working experience in the industry. The survey indicated that individuals with work experience of five to nine years only, formed 31% of the survey responses. Only 7% of respondents held over 30 years working experience in the construction industry.

The survey required the participants to indicate their academic qualifications; the project team had different role players and the research aimed to ensure that all the project team members from various disciplines participated in the survey. This ensured eliminating bias, by confirming that not only project managers would respond to the survey. The requirement for the qualification identification in the survey, verified that engineers, planners, SHE officers and quality inspectors, amongst others, also participated in the questionnaire survey. The aim was to provide the study more credibility, whilst covering a wide range.

5.2   Section B: The Role of Project Managers in Project Management

Various authors and researchers in the literature review, postulate that some of the project delay causes could be avoided if project managers were proactive, suggesting that project managers are to blame partly for some delays in construction projects.

This section was added to the questionnaire with the aim of seeking to understand the general perception of the project role players and project stake holders on the role of project managers in traction substation projects and whether they are fulfilling their duties.

5.3   Section C: Causes of Project Delays

The literature review identified the following project delay causes:

- Scope changes.
- Design changes during construction.
- Unavailability of the client for supervision/oversight/approval.
- Shortage of project resources.
- Constricted construction schedules.
- External interference, such as politics and weather.
- Land acquisition.
- Payment difficulties.

Various studies in the past such as Oshungade and Kruger (2016), alluded to the labour unrests as one of the delay causing factors in construction projects. However, for the duration of this research the labour unrests were not experienced, in the specific areas where this research was conducted on PRASA and Transnet infrastructure development projects. This suggest that this problem is not experienced regurlary on the traction substation projects.

The purpose of introducing this section to the questionnaire was to establish how frequently the aforementioned project delay causes are encountered in construction projects, particularly in traction substation construction projects. Higher numbers of respondents, indicating 35%, specified limited experience of scenarios where the client fails to pay the contractor timeously for the work. Only 5% of the results identified certain projects with payment challenges.

External interferences, such as weather and politics were also identified from the literature reviews as causes for project delays. This did not seem to be a significant challenge for Transnet and PRASA, since these interferences only affect their projects at certain intervals.

From the literature review, scope changes were identified as some of the most general project delay-causing factors. Yang and Wei (2010); Yang, Chu *et al.* (2013) and Chanmeka, Thomas *et al.* (2012) listed scope changes as delay factors in their respective elements. Based on the feedback from the questionnaire survey, it indicates that from 83 survey responses, 33 (40%) indicated that scope changes are experienced often in construction projects, hindering the progress of the project. Nine individuals (11%) indicated that they always experienced delays due to scope changes in all their project involvements.

A mere 6% of respondents indicated that they have never experienced project delays caused by scope changes. This aspect suggest the clients' awareness of the requirements. Contractors and consultants therefore complied with all the contract requirements.

Elawi, Algahtany and Kashiwagi (2016); Chanmeka, Thomas *et al.* (2012); Zidane and Andersen (2018), and Parsons (2015) (in their respective publications), included the design changes during construction amongst the project delay-causing factors. The survey results emphasised theory indicated in the literature; over 40% of respondents attested that they encountered delays in their daily running of projects; as a result, the progress of the project was often affected.

The majority of participants' (37%) responses observed that the client was often available when required for supervision, oversight or approval of documents and designs. The impression is that clients were unavailable at times; more than 8% expressed that they never encountered a situation where the client was absent, delaying the project.

The survey results did not entirely correlate with the Yang, Chu *et al.* (2013); Srdic and Selih (2015) and Doloi, Sawhney *et al.* (2012), whereby they label the unavailability of the client as one of the top delay-causing factors in construction projects. The perception is that it is a delay-causing factor, but on these traction substation projects, PRASA and Transnet employees as the clients, were usually available when required.

The shortage of project resources was also emphasised to cause delays in construction projects (Zidane and Andersen, 2018; Parsons, 2015). The results show that the majority of respondents sensed that only at certain times the project was delayed due to a shortage of project resources. This information suggests that project managers in these projects, performed their duties well, allocating project resources; 36% of respondents indicated that they did not often experience delays due to resource shortages.

Similar to project resource shortages, it might be due to proper planning by the project team in traction substation projects; 33 of 83 respondents submitted that their projects were delayed due to squeezed construction schedules, only at certain times; 29% indicated that they often encountered a 'squeezed' schedule and 12% also submitted that they were always confronted with construction delays due to schedule challenges. Rentschler *et al.* (2017) and Zidane and Andersen (2018) confirmed this theory.

Ansah and Sorooshian (2018), Hussain et al. (2017), Yang, Chu et al. (2013), Stoudt (2013) and Parsons (2015), are the authors who mainly discussed the theory of external interference in construction projects caused by factors, such as politics and weather amongst others.

The perception from these authors is that delay-causing factors outside the control of the project team exist. The project team needs to consider these during the planning stages of the project. Approximately 39% of the responses sense that delays due to external interferences are experienced at times; 30% indicated that they always encountered delays due to external interferences. Only a mere 2% expressed that they have never encountered delays due to external interferences in the project.

Elawi, Algahtany and Kashiwagi (2016) identify land acquisition as one of the delay-causing factors in construction projects. The survey results confirmed that construction projects encounter this challenge; 17 % indicated that it occurred often; 24% suggested that it occurred rarely. The majority of the respondents (38%) encountered land acquisition challenges occasionally.

PRASA and Transnet seem to be reliable, since the questionnaire findings revealed that approximately 35% of respondents claim to have rarely encountered a situation where the client failed to process the contractor payment for a completed project.

5.4   Section D: Recommended Mitigations

The last part of the questionnaire was Section D, where the focus area aimed to determine (from the participants) the more suitable recommended mitigations and remedial actions to be implemented to manage project delays in construction projects, particularly traction substation projects.

Respondents were expected to indicate their views according to the following Likert scale:

1   = Strongly Disagree (SD).

2   = Disagree (D).

3   = Neutral (N).

4   = Agree (A).

5   = Strongly Agree (SA).

This indicated the extent of agreeing or disagreeing with the mitigation, proposed in the questionnaire.

It is evident from the reviewed literature that numerous studies posit that it may not be possible to avoid delays completely; there are some suitable mitigations that could be implemented to manage them. Parsons (2015) proposes the following mitigations to manage delays in construction projects:

- Appoint experienced and reputable contractors and consultants.
- Do not appoint a contractor based on the lowest bid price only.
- More involvement of the engineering team is recommended in projects to ensure complete and quality designs.

The feedback received, revealed that most of respondents either agree or strongly agree with proposed mitigations; 45% of respondents agree, whilst 33% strongly agree that it would be in the best interest of the project if the designers could request involvement of the construction team, during the process of developing the engineering designs.

Zidane and Andersen (2018) propose that reliable engineering ethics and accountability should be promoted and encouraged, especially amongst the designers and the construction team; 67% of respondents strongly agree with these mitigations and 31% agree. There were no disagreements captured; only 1 of the survey participants were undecided.

Understanding laws, rules and regulations that could hinder the project, was a mitigation that were presented (Stoudt, 2013). An overwhelming 47% agree and 46% strongly agree that this mitigation needs to be implemented to manage delays in construction projects; 4% of respondents were undecided and equally, 4% disagreed with the proposed mitigation.

A mitigation well received by respondents, was to ensure that the planning teams and engineering teams worked on a similar project as previously undertaken. A combination of responses that agree and strongly agree with implementing this mitigation, indicated 75% of the responses received, supporting theory shared by the study.

Rentschler *et al.* (2017) suggest implementing the following mitigation in construction projects to manage delays:

- Timely project planning is encouraged.
- Run independent construction activities in parallel.
- Allow for contingency.
- Involve the construction team in engineering processes, such as designs.
- Organise labourers accordingly.

The survey participants sensed that it would expedite the construction activities if independent activities in construction projects could run parallel or simultaneously; 55% agree, whilst 25% strongly agreed with the proposed mitigation.

5.5   Chapter Summary

A comparison between the literature reviews covered in Chapter 2 and data presentation and analysis in Chapter 4, posited a correlation. The questionnaire survey results corresponded with the statements by various authors in their respective articles in the literature review.

The project delay-causing factors that were identified by the authors, were revealed to be relevant as the questionnaire requested the frequency that the project team encountered delay-causing factors. Most of respondents indicated that they encounter them daily in their project administration. The proposed mitigations from literature were well received by the survey participants.

Chapter 6

Conclusions and Recommendations

6.1   Introduction

This chapter intends to assist the reader to understand the importance of the research, after perusing the study. A conclusion in this study does not merely indicate a summary of the main topics covered or a re-statement of the research problem, but a synthesis of crucial factors. The significance of this study indicates researching a global challenge of delays in construction projects. Delays continue to worsen. The study gained an in-depth underlying theoretical understanding of the subject.

6.2   Conclusion

Delays affect several construction projects in South Africa and globally. History suggest that project delays were always part of construction projects. The difference between the past and the present is the accelerated rate of the project delays.

Delays in the construction environment are categorised into excusable delays. These delays are caused by external interferences, such as weather and politics. They are also classified into the category of non-excusable delays. The prescribed processes and procedures were not followed in some phases of the project.

Some projects are simple; they may be completed in a brief period and without difficulties. Certain projects are complex and are extended over long intervals.

Various authors from the reviewed literature, posit that delays in construction projects have negative implications on the economy of several countries globally; the construction industry is one of the largest contributors to the GDP of several countries.

The questionnaire survey respondents agreed and validated the identified project delay factors as indicated in the literature review. The most general project delay-causing factors in traction substation projects were identified; suitable mitigations were recommended in this study.

Several researchers established that project delays are not peculiar in the project engineering environment, but that they are common. Delays vary from project to project; it could be hours, days, weeks or even years. That does not necessarily indicate the extend of the financial loss incurred. It is possible that the project that was delayed by a few hours, suffered a severe financial setback, additional to a project suspended for a year.

Figure 28 below shows the delay-causing factors according to the survey results, indicating the most and the least general delay causes.

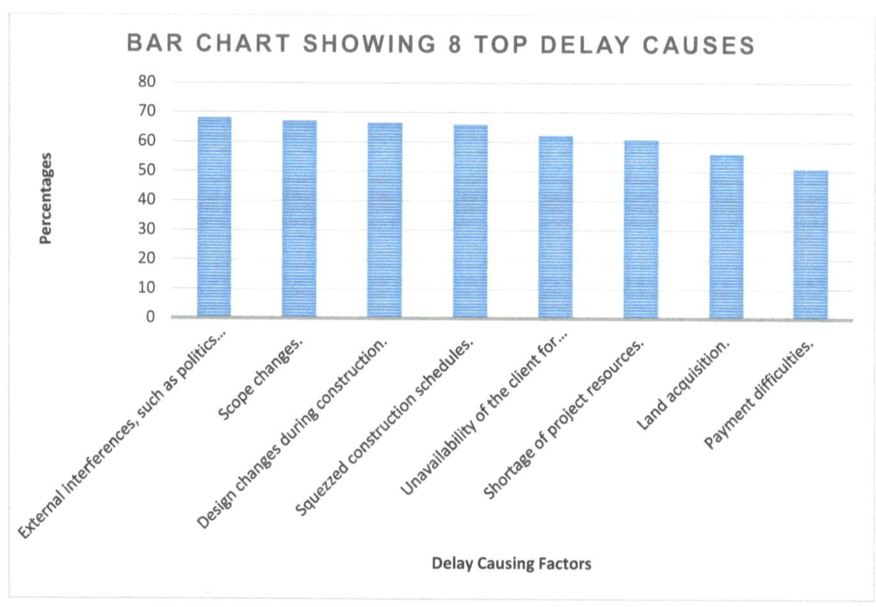

Figure 26: Top 8 delay-causing factors

6.3   Recommendations

A general viewpoint for several authors and researchers is that it may not be possible to avoid delays completely. Recommendable remedial actions and suitable mitigations are available that could be introduced and implemented in construction projects to manage project delays.

The feedback from the research questionnaire and the literature review, recommends the following measures for project management implementation to manage project delays:

- Efficient project managers should not micro-manage their project team; they need to let them freely express themselves. They need to assess them, based on their productivity.

- The good traits of a good project manager indicate proactive planning and timeous identification of potential delay risks.
- To expedite construction projects, it is advisable to run independent construction activities concurrently.
- An efficient project manager needs to manage scope changes or scope creeps, imposed on the project by the client.

The research suggested the following mitigations to be suitable to manage project delays in construction projects, particularly traction substation projects:

- Proactive planning and timeous identification of potential delay risks.
- Running of independent construction activities in parallel.
- Involving construction teams in the engineering processes, such as designs.
- Ensuring that planning and engineering teams hold experience, similar to the planned project.
- Understanding of laws, rules and regulations that could hinder the project.
- Ensuring availability of project funding, prior to the construction commencement.
- Preparing a detailed construction plan.
- Appointing experienced and reputable contractors and consultants.
- Refraining from appointing a contractor, based on the lowest bid price only.
- Promoting good engineering ethics and accountability.
- Adhering to the set milestones.

6.4 Suggestion for Further Research

This research did not cover the negative financial implications as a consequence of project delays in construction projects (for traction substation in particular). It would be beneficial to calculate construction projects' financial losses, based on the project delay factors discussed in this study.

References

Abedian, I., October 2003. Executive Summary Transnet. *Asia Africa Intelligence Wire.*

Abd IL-Karim, M.S.B., El Nawawy, O.A.M., and Abdel-Alim, A.M., 2017. Identification and assessment of risk factors affecting construction projects. *HBRC Journal,* **13**(2), pp. 202-216.

Abdul-Rahman, H., Berawi, M.A., Berawi, A.R., Mohamed, O., Othman, M. and Yahya, I.A., 2006. Delay Mitigation in the Malaysian Construction Industry. *Journal of Construction Engineering and Management,* **132**(2), pp. 125-133.

Abdul-Rahman, H., Takim, R. and Min, W.S., 2009. Financial-related causes contributing to project delays. *Journal of Retail and Leisure Property,* **8**(3), pp. 225-238.

Agyekum-Mensah, G., and Knight, A.D., 2017. The professionals' perspective on project delay in the construction industry. *Engineering, Construction and Architectural Management,* **24**(5), pp. 828-841.

Ali, A.S. and Rahmat, I., 2010. The performance measurement of construction projects managed by ISO-certified contractors in Malaysia. *Journal of Retail and Leisure Property,* **9**(1), pp. 25-35.

Alinaitwe, H., Apolot, R., and Tindiwensi, D., 2013. Investigation into the cause of Delays and Cost Overruns in Uganda's Public Sector Construction Projects. *Journal of Construction in Developing Countries,* **18**(2), pp. 33.

Alzara, M., Kashiwagi, D., Kashiwagi, J. and Al-Tassan, A., 2016. Using PIPS to Minimise Causes of Delay in Saudi Arabian Construction Projects: University Case Study. *Procedia Engineering,* **145**, pp. 932-939.

Aminah, f., Manjula, D., and Oswaldo, C., 2004. Developing a standard methodology for measuring and classifying construction field rework. *Canadian Journal of Civil Engineering,* **31**(6), pp. 1077-1089.

Amoatey, C.T., and Alfred Ankrah, A.N.O, 2017. Exploring critical road project delay factors in Ghana. *Journal of Facilities Management,* **15**(2), pp. 110-127.

Ansah, R.H., and Sorooshian, S., 2018. 4P delays in project management. *Engineering, Construction and Architectural Management,* **25**(1), pp. 62-76.

Aziz, R.F., 2013. Ranking of delay factors in construction projects after Egyptian revolution. *Alexandria Engineering Journal,* **52**(3), pp. 387-406.

Basak, M., Coffey, V. and Perrons, R.K., 2017. Exploring risks causing schedule overrun in upstream natural gas projects - A critical review and implications for future research, 2017, IEEE, pp. 730-734.

Bastianelli, L.A., Yeager, T., Wolf, B.D., and Fultineer, R.D., 2012. Project Development and Strategies for Success, *Berkeley Research Group,* pp. 1-12.

Chanmeka, A., Thomas, S.R., Caldas, C.H. and Mulva, S.P., 2012. Assessing crucial factors impacting the performance and productivity of oil and gas projects in Alberta. *Canadian Journal of Civil Engineering,* **39**(3), pp. 259-270.

Chan, P.C., Chan, D.W.M., Chiang, Y.H.,Tang, B.S., Chan, E.H.W and Ho, K.S.K., 2004. Exploring Critical Success Factors for Partnering in Construction Projects, Journal *Of Construction Engineering And Management* © *Asce,* pp. 188-198.

Das, D.K., and Emuze, F., 2017. A Dynamic Model of Contractor-Induced Delays in India. *Journal of Construction in Developing Countries,* **22**(1), pp. 21-39.

Dickson, E.B., and Whitehurst, R., 2016. Integrated Project Planning in a Construction Management Environment: The College of DuPage's Naperville, Illinois, Satellite Campus. *Planning for Higher Education,* **45**(1), pp. 160.

Doloi, H., Sawhney, A. and Iyer, K.C., 2012. Structural equation model for investigating factors affecting delay in Indian construction projects. *Construction Management and Economics,* **30**(10), pp. 869-884.

Duke, P., 2015. Project Success Factors. Considerations that apply to all delivery models. *Health facilities management,* **28**(8), pp. 28.

Elawi, G.S.A., Algahtany, M. and Kashiwagi, D., 2016. Owners' Perspective of Factors Contributing to Project Delay: Case Studies of Road and Bridge Projects in Saudi Arabia. *Procedia Engineering,* **145**, pp. 1402-1409.

Faridi, A.S. and El-Sayegh, S.M., 2006. Significant factors causing delay in the UAE construction industry. *Construction Management and Economics,* **24**(11), pp. 1167-1176.

Fink, A., "How to Conduct Surveys", 3rd Edition; Alan Aldridge; Kevin Levine, *"Surveying the Social World"*

Gardezi, S.S.S., Manarvi, I.A. and Gardezi, S.J.S., 2014. Time Extension Factors in the construction industry of Pakistan. *Procedia Engineering,* **77**, pp. 196-204.

Gluszak, m. and Lesniak., 2015. Construction delays in client's opinion - multivariate statistical. *Creative Construction Conference 2015 (CCC2015), Procedia Engineering,* pp. 182-189.

Hussain, S., Zhu, F., Ali, Z., and Xu, X., 2017. Rural Residents' Perception of Construction Project Delays in Pakistan. *Sustainability,* **9**(11), pp. 2108.

Hussain. S., Zhu, F., Ali, Z., Aslam, H.D., and Hussain, A., 2018. Critical Delaying Factors: Public Sector Building Projects in Gilgit-Baltistan, Pakistan. *Buildings,* **8**(1), pp. 6.

Idoro, G., 2012. Comparing levels of use of project plans and performance of traditional contract and design-build construction projects in Nigeria. *Journal of Engineering, Design and Technology,* **10**(1), pp. 7-33.

Islam, A., Al Owad, A. M. M, Badraig, O.M., Ma, l. and Karim, M.A., 2014a. Factors affecting new project delays in Saudi Arabian manufacturing organisations, 2014, IEEE, pp. 381-386.

Kazaz, A., Ulubeyli, S. and Tuncbilekli, N.A., 2012. Causes of Delays in Construction Projects in Turkey. *Journal of Civil Engineering and Management,* **18**(3), pp. 426-435.

Khan, R.A. and Gul, W., 2017. Empirical study of critical risk factors causing delays in construction projects, 2017, IEEE, pp. 900-906.

Leung, W., 2001. How to design a questionnaire. *Student BMJ,* **9**, pp. 187.

Lo, T.Y., Fung, I.W.H. and Tung, K.C.F., 2006. Construction Delays in Hong Kong Civil Engineering Projects. *Journal of Construction Engineering and Management,* **132**(6), pp. 636-649.

Marks, M. G. and Ellis. A. E., 2013. Delays in Major Agricultural Infrastructure Projects in Guyana: Causes and Proposed solutions. The Westen Indian Journal of Engineering, pp. 79-85.

McCusker, K. and Gunaydin, S., 2015. Research using qualitative, quantitative or mixed methods and choice based on the research. *Perfusion,* **30**(7), pp. 537-542.

Miller, D., Pearsall, E., Johnston, D., Frecea, M. and Mckenzie, M., 2017. Executive Summary. *Journal of Wound, Ostomy and Continence Nursing,* **44**(1), pp. 74-77.

Milne, J., 2010. Questionnaire: Some Advantages and Disadvantages. *Centre for CBL in Land Use and Environmental Sciences, Aberdeen University.* Available online: http://orangegrouprsmet.blogspot.com/2010/11/advantages-disadvantages-of.html

Nielsen, Y., Özdemir, M. and Gündüz, M., 2013. Quantification of Delay Factors Using the Relative Importance Index Method for Construction Projects in Turkey. *Journal of Management in Engineering,* **29**(2), pp. 133-139.

Nkobane, M.A., 2012. Causes of delay and cost overruns in engineering, procurement and construction management projects in South Africa, M.S. thesis, Dept. Eng. Manage., Univ. Johannesburg, South Africa.

Oakland. J.S., and Marosszeky, M., 2017a. *Total Construction Management.* London: Routledge Ltd - M.U.A.

Ofori-Kuragu,J.K., Owusu-Manu, D and Joshua Ayarkwa,J., 2016. The Case for a Construction Industry Council in Ghana. *Journal of Construction in Developing Countries,* **21**(2), pp. 131.

Oshungane O.O and Kruger D, 2016. A comparative study of causes and effects of project delays and disruptions in construction projects in the South African Construction industry: City of Johannesburg as a case study.

Parsons, B., 2015. Large construction projects are taking years longer than they're supposed to — and the public want to know why. *Delays, Getty Images, Canadian Consulting Engineers,* pp. 23-29.

Questionnaire design, Topic 9. *Deakin University.*

R.D. Olson Construction, 2014. Congratulations, *B-60 orange county business journal, Kana Pipeline, inc,* pp. 1.

Rao, B.P., Shekar, S.C., Jaiswal, N., Jain, A., and Saxena, A.D., 2016. Delay Analysis of Construction Projects. *Journal of Information Technology and Economic Development,* **7**(1), pp. 15

Rentschler., C. Engineering Consultant, Akron, Pennsylvania, G. Shahani, Shureline Construction inc., Kenton and Delaware, *HP Special Focus Plant Design, Engineering and Construction.*

Swinson, R., Clark, A.C., Ernst, J.V., and Sutton, K., 2016. New roles for project design engineers. *Technology and Engineering Teacher,* **75**(8), pp. 8.

Samarghandi, H., Tabatabaei, S.M.M., Taabayan, P., Hashemi, A.M. and Willoughby, K., 2016. Studying the Reasons for Delay and Cost Overrun in Construction Projects: The Case of Iran. *Journal of Construction in Developing Countries,* **21**(1), pp. 51-84.

Saunders, M., Lewis, P., and Thornhill, A., 2012. Research Methods for Business Students, *6th Edition, England: Pearson Limited,* 2012.

Skinner, M., 2010. Research - the essential guide, Ways to categorise research and methodology. Available online: https://www.scribd.com/document/35577412/Film-Research-the-Essential-Guide

Srdic, A., and Selih, J., 2015. Delays in Construction Projects: Causes and Mitigation. *Organisation, Technology and Management in Construction,* **7**(3).

Soliman, E., 2017. Communication Problems Causing Governmental Projects Delay. kuwait case study. *Global Journal of Construction project management,* **9**(1), pp. 55-71.

Spalek, S. (2005). Critical success factors in project management. To fail or not to fail, that is the question! Paper presented at PMI® Global Congress 2005—EMEA, Edinburgh, Scotland. Newtown Square, PA: Project Management Institute.

South African Railway Network, 2004. *Transnet Freight Rail,* Drawing: BBB8097, Sheet 1 of 1.

Sweis, R., Sweis, G., Abu Hammad, A. and Shboul, A., 2008. Delays in construction projects: The case of Jordan. *Global Journal of project management,* **26**(6), pp. 665-674.

Venkateswaran C.B. and Murugasan. R., 2017. Time Delay and Cost Overrun of Road over Bridge (ROB) Construction Projects in India. *Journal of Construction in Developing Countries,* **22**, pp. 79-96.

Venkitachalam, R., 2015. Validity and Reliability of Questionnaire. Available: https://www.slideshare.net/Venkitachalam/validity-and-reliability-of-questionnaires

Williams, T., 2016. Identifying Success Factors in Construction Projects: A Case Study. *Project Management Journal,* **47**(1), pp. 97-112.

Yang, J., Chu, M. and Huang, K., 2013. An Empirical Study of Schedule Delay Causes Based on Taiwan's Litigation Cases. *Project Management Journal,* **44**(3), pp. 21-31.

Yang, J. and Wei, P., 2010. Causes of Delay in the Planning and Design Phases for Construction Projects. *Journal of Architectural Engineering,* **16**(2), pp. 80-83.

Wang, H. and Hubbarb, H., 2017. A survey study on industrial construction project supply. *Creative Construction Conference, Procedia Engineering*, pp. 653-659

Zakaria, S.F, Zin, R.M., Mohammed, I., Bulabaid, S and Rahim E.M.R., 2017. Critical Success Factors in Infrastructure Projects. *Proceedings of the 3rd International Conference on Construction and Building Engineering (ICONBUILD)*, pp 1-8

Zidane, Y.J.T., and Andersen, B., 2018. Delay and their cures in major Norwegian projects. *Norwegian University of Technology and Science.* Vol 5.

* 9 7 8 9 9 7 5 1 5 4 2 4 6 *